World of Science

A–Z of Essential Terms

OXFORD

World of Science

A–Z of Essential Terms

BRIAN DEUTROM
GEORGE BETHELL

OXFORD
UNIVERSITY PRESS

OXFORD
UNIVERSITY PRESS

Great Clarendon Street, Oxford OX2 6DP
Oxford University Press is a department of the University of Oxford.
It furthers the University's objective of excellence in research, scholarship,
and education by publishing worldwide in

Oxford New York

Athens Auckland Bangkok Bogotá Buenos Aires Calcutta
Cape Town Chennai Dar es Salaam Delhi Florence Hong Kong Istanbul
Karachi Kuala Lumpur Madrid Melbourne Mexico City Mumbai Nairobi
Paris São Paulo Singapore Taipei Tokyo Toronto Warsaw

with associated companies in Berlin Ibadan

OXFORD is a registered trade mark of Oxford University Press
in the UK and certain other countries

© Brian Deutrom and George Bethell 1999

First published 1999

All rights reserved. No part of this publication may be reproduced,
stored in a retrieval system, or transmitted, in any form or by any means,
without the prior permission in writing of Oxford University Press, or as
expressly permitted by law, or under terms agreed with the
appropriate reprographics rights organisation. Enquiries concerning
reproduction outside the scope of the above should be sent to the
Rights Department, Oxford University Press, at the above address.
You must not circulate this book in any other binding or cover
and you must impose this same condition on any acquirer.

British Library Cataloguing in Publication Data.
Data available
ISBN 0 19 551152 2

Edited by Barry Stone
Illustrated by Juli Kent
Cover and text design by Caroline Laird
Typeset by Stephen Chan
Printed through Bookpac Production Services, Singapore
Published by Oxford University Press

Preface

This compact book aims to provide a comprehensive list of the most important terms you are likely to meet in your science courses. It covers the essential words and phrases for Key Stage 3 of the National Curriculum and for all GCSE syllabuses.

Each entry contains a basic definition, followed, where appropriate, by a more detailed explanation or example. Not only is the word defined, but other words related to the topic are indicated. For example, **evolution** leads you to **Darwinism** which leads to **natural selection** which leads to **artificial selection**. Highlighting the connection between words in this way allows you to gain a more thorough understanding—especially when revising for examinations.

An easy-to-use pronunciation guide is given for words that are hard to pronounce or difficult to recognise. The word is broken up into small units. These are shown in square brackets with the part you need to stress printed in bold type. For example: **haemoglobin** [heem-o-**gloh**-bin].

The dictionary contains, in addition to over 1300 entries, many diagrams to help you visualise and understand important topics. At the back there are appendices which you can use to look up information and data. For example, Appendix A is the Periodic Table of the Elements.

We hope that by using this reference book you will find it easier to understand the terminology of science and that this, in turn, will help you to be successful in your studies.

Brian Deutrom
George Bethell
1999

abdomen [ab-de-men]
1 the part of an animal's body containing the stomach, intestines and other digestive organs such as the liver.
2 the rear part of an insect behind the thorax or chest.

abort [a-bort]
to end something before it has been completed, such as aborting a space flight because of problems.

abortion [a-bor-shn]
removal of an embryo from the womb before it has developed enough to survive.

absolute zero
the same as zero Kelvin, 0K, or –273°C. It is the lowest possible temperature because the particles in an object have the lowest possible kinetic energy; they are stationary.

absorb
1 to soak up or take in, e.g. the roots of a plant absorb water from the soil.
2 to receive something and reduce its effect, e.g. shock absorbers reduce the vibrations in a car.

absorption
any process by which a dissolved substance passes through a membrane into a living organism.

a.c.
abbreviation for alternating current. See **alternating current**.

accelerate
to go faster. See **decelerate**.

acceleration
the rate at which the velocity of an object changes.

$$\text{accel}^{n.} = \frac{\text{change of velocity}}{\text{time}}$$

accumulator
a battery for storing electricity, such as those used in cars. Solar panels can be used to charge accumulators to provide energy in remote areas. See **lead-acid cell**.

acetic acid
[a-**see**-tik a-sid]
an organic acid also known as ethanoic acid CH_3COOH. A weak solution is called vinegar and used to flavour and preserve food.

acid
a substance that is soluble in water, contains hydrogen, and can neutralise a base. Acids turn litmus red, and have a pH of less than 7. Acids form positively charged hydronium (hydroxonium) ions H_3O^+ in a solution in water. See **pH**, **strong acid**, **weak acid**.

acid rain
form of air pollution caused when acidic oxides, e.g. sulphur dioxide gas from power stations and factories, dissolve in moisture in the air, making acids. Acid rain damages buildings and trees. It can also kill wildlife in lakes and ponds.

acid reactions
acids react with metals to produce hydrogen H_2, with marble chips (calcium carbonate, $CaCO_3$) and other carbonate compounds to produce carbon dioxide CO_2, and with bases to produce salts and water.

acquired immunity
1 natural immunity from a disease, resulting from having had the disease in the past.
2 artificial immunity from a disease, resulting from vaccination.
See **immunity**.

action and reaction
a pair of equal and opposite forces.

active immunity
see **immunize**.

active transport
the movement of dissolved substances across a cell membrane from regions of low concentration to regions of high concentration. This process uses energy produced by respiration. See **diffusion**.

adaptation
a change in organisms that makes them better suited to a particular environment. See **natural selection**.

addition polymerisation
[a-di-shn pol-im-er-ryz-a-shn]
chemical reaction during which molecules of the same

type link to form new, long, chain-like molecules.

adolescence [ad-o-**less**-ens]
that period in life in humans that usually occurs in the early teenage years. It is the period between the end of childhood and full adult maturity. See **puberty**.

adrenaline [a-**dren**-a-lyn]
hormone released by the adrenal gland when humans and other animals are frightened or angry. It prepares the body for action by speeding up breathing and heart beat. See **fight-or-flight**.

aerial [air-ree-ul]
wire, rod or dish used to transmit and receive the electromagnetic radiation used for radio, TV, mobile phone signals. See **antenna**.

aerobic respiration
[air-oh-bic **ress**-pir-a-shn]
respiration that takes place inside cells to produce energy by using oxygen. Glucose is changed to carbon dioxide and water. See **respiration**.

afterbirth
see **placenta**.

agar [ay-gar]
a jelly-like starch extracted from seaweed. It is used in the laboratory to grow bacteria.

agriculture
the study and practice of cultivating land for the growing of crops and the rearing of livestock.

AIDS
a disease that greatly weakens a person's ability to resist infections. The word comes from the first letters of 'acquired immune deficiency syndrome'. See **safer sex**.

air
a mixture of gases that surround the Earth and which most living things breathe. Air is mainly nitrogen (78%) and oxygen (21%).

air pollution
the release of substances into the atmosphere that have harmful effects on the environment. See **acid rain**, **greenhouse effect**, **pollution**.

air pressure
the force exerted by the weight of air particles on any unit of surface area. See **barometer**.

air resistance
frictional force which acts against a body moving through air.

airship
a large, helium-filled balloon with engines, used to carry passengers and goods.

albino
animal or human lacking the natural body colours in the eyes, skin and hair. This is an inherited characteristic.

alchemist [al-ka-mist]
a person who lived in the twelfth to the seventeenth centuries, and who tried to turn ordinary metals into gold. The word comes from the Arabic language, 'al-kimiya' meaning the art of changing metals. 'Al-kimiya' is the origin of the word chemistry.

alcohol
1. a type of organic compound containing an –OH group attached to a hydrocarbon. The simplest alcohol is methanol CH_3OH. Ethanol C_2H_5OH and propanol C_3H_7OH are the next two alcohols in the series.
2. a common name for ethanol. See **ethanol**.

alcohol fermentation
a respiration process of certain yeasts and bacteria during which carbohydrates such as sugars or starch are broken down to release energy. Alcohol (ethanol C_2H_5OH) and carbon dioxide are by-products.

algae [al-gee]
simple organisms that live in water or in moist places on land. They have no leaves, roots, or stems. They contain chlorophyll and therefore carry out photosynthesis.

alimentary canal [al-i-**ment**-er-i]
a tube in animals through which food is taken in and digested. The useful components are absorbed and the waste is eliminated. Most animals have a hole at each end of the tube. See **coelenterate**. See **Fig. 1** (p. 5).

alkali [al-ka-ly]
a substance that is soluble in water and can neutralise an acid. Alkalis are bases that form negatively charged hydroxide ions OH^- in solution in water. See **base**.

alkali metals
group 1 of elements in the periodic table that all have one electron in their outer shell. They are lithium Li, sodium Na, potassium K, rubidium Rb, caesium Cs, and francium Fr. They react violently with water to form hydrogen gas and alkali hydroxides.

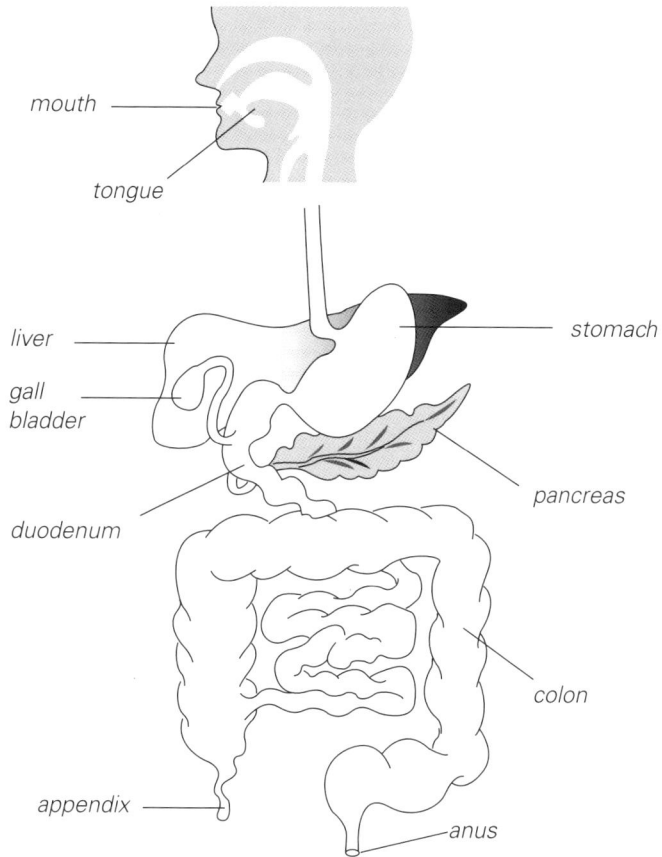

Fig. 1 the human alimentary canal

alkaline

a basic solution that has a pH of more than 7, turns red litmus blue and contains an excess of hydroxide OH⁻ ions. See **basic**.

alkaline earth metals

elements of group 2 of the periodic table including magnesium Mg and calcium Ca. They react with water to give hydrogen but are less reactive than the group 1 metals. See **alkali metals**.

alkane [al-kay-n]

organic compound containing carbon atoms joined to hydrogen atoms by single bonds only. The simplest alkane is methane CH_4. Alkanes are good fuels.

alkene [al-keen]
organic compound, containing only carbon and hydrogen atoms, in which two of the carbon atoms are joined by a double bond. See **alkane**.

allele [al-el]
a particular form of a gene. For example, brown, green and blue are alleles of the gene for eye colour. See **gene**.

allergy [al-er-ji]
a condition in which antibodies produced by the body in response to antigens such as dust, pollen or certain foods actually harm the body. Asthma and hay fever are allergic reactions.

allotrope [al-o-trohp]
different forms of the same element that have different structures and different physical properties. Diamonds and graphite are allotropes of carbon.

alloy [al-oi]
a metal formed by mixing two or more metals. Brass is an alloy of copper and zinc. Stainless steel is iron mixed with small amounts of chromium, manganese and nickel.

alluvial soil [a-loo-vi-al]
a soil formed from material deposited by rivers.

alpha particle
[al-fa **par**-ti-kal]
a positively charged particle, consisting of two protons and two neutrons, that is given off when some radioactive elements decay.

alpha radiation
[al-fa **ray**-di-**ay**-shn]
a stream of alpha particles moving at about 1/10th the speed of light. Alpha radiation cannot penetrate a sheet of thick paper.

alternating current
[awl-ter-nay-ting]
an electric current that reverses its direction with constant frequency. The 'mains' electricity supplied to homes from power stations is alternating current. See **a.c., electric current**.

alternator [awl-ter-nay-ter]
a generator consisting of a coil or coils that rotate in a magnetic field and produce alternating current.

aluminium
symbol Al. A light-weight, silver-coloured metallic element Z=13. Used in the manufacture of aeroplanes and cooking pots.

alveolus [al-vee-oh-lus]
small air sac (pl. alveoli) in the lungs, through which oxygen and carbon dioxide

pass in and out of the surrounding blood capillaries. See **gas exchange**, **lung**.

amino acid [a-**mee**-no a-sid]
a group of organic compounds that contain nitrogen and are the building blocks that join together in chains to form proteins.

ammeter [**am**-ee-ter]
an instrument used to measure electric current.

ammonia [a-**moh**-ni-a]
a strong smelling gas NH_3, that forms the base ammonium hydroxide NH_4OH, in solution in water.

ammonite [**am**-o-nyte]
an example of an index fossil. See **index fossil**.

amnion [**am**-ni-on]
a membrane that encloses the embryo of reptiles, birds and mammals, providing protection to the developing foetus.

amoeba [a-**mee**-ba]
a microscopic, one-celled animal that lives in water and constantly changes shape.

amoebic dysentery [a-**mee**-bic **dis**-en-tree] a severe gastro-intestinal disease caused by a species of amoeba found in polluted water.

ampere [**am**-pair]
symbol A. The unit for measuring electric current.

Amphibia
the amphibians.

amphibian [am-**fib**-i-an]
cold-blooded animal that is born in water with gills, but later develops lungs and lives on land, e.g. frog. Vertebrate of the class Amphibia.

amplifier
an instrument that increases the strength of an electric signal. Amplifiers are used in radios and electronic instruments to make sounds louder.

amplitude [**amp**-lee-chewd]
the size of a wave. If a sound wave produces a loud noise it has a large amplitude.

amylase [**am**-i-layz]
a group of enzymes that helps break down starch into glucose and other sugars. An amylase enzyme is found in human saliva.

anaemia [a-**nee**-mi-a]
a sickness caused by a lack of red blood cells. It is common when there is not enough iron in the diet. Many pregnant women taken iron supplements to avoid anaemia.

anaerobic bacteria [an-air-**oh**-bik bac-**teer**-i-a]
organisms that obtain energy through anaerobic respiration. They break down the waste in sewage systems.

anaerobic respiration [an-air-**oh**-bik ress-pir-ay-shn]
respiration that takes place inside cells to produce energy without using oxygen. Yeast and many bacteria use anaerobic respiration.

anaesthetic [an-iss-**thet**-ik]
a local anaesthetic is a chemical that causes a loss of feeling in one area of the body. General anaesthetics cause total unconsciousness.

analyse
1 to separate something into its parts.
2 to examine and interpret something.

anemone [a-**nem**-o-nee]
a simple animal from the group coelenterates (jellyfish). It lives in the sea, attaches itself to rocks, and looks like a plant.

aneroid barometer [an-er-oid ba-**rom**-it-er]
a device for measuring atmospheric pressure, consisting of a thin metal box from which air has been removed, connected to a scale pointer. Changes in air pressure cause the top of the box and, hence, the pointer to move. See **barometer.**

angiosperm [**an**-ji-o-sperm]
the group name for the flowering plants.

angle of incidence
the angle between a ray falling on a surface and the perpendicular (normal) to the surface. See **reflection, refraction**.

angle of reflection
the angle between a ray leaving a reflecting surface and the perpendicular (normal) to the surface. See **reflection**.

angle of refraction
the angle between a ray that is refracted at a surface between two different media and the perpendicular (normal) to the surface. See **refraction**.

anhydrous [an-**hy**-drus]
a chemical compound lacking in water, such as

anhydrous copper sulphate $CuSO_4$ that has lost its water of crystallisation.

animal
a living thing that is not a plant. Animals cannot make their own food, but have to feed on plants and other animals. Most animals can move from place to place. There are many groups of animals.

anion [an-i-on]
a negatively charged ion. Non-metal atoms gain electrons to form anions, e.g. chlorine atoms gain one electron to form Cl^- anions. Anions are attracted to the anode during electrolysis. See **anode, cation, cell, electrolysis.**

annelid [an-il-id]
the group name for worms such as earthworms and leeches whose bodies are divided into segments.

annual
a plant that completes its life cycle in one year during which it germinates, flowers, produces seeds and dies.

anode [an-ohd]
a positively charged electrode. In a cell, the anode attracts electrons back into the cell to maintain the electric current. During electrolysis, the negatively charged ions (anions) are attracted to the anode. See **anion, cathode, cell, electrolysis.**

Anopheles [a-nof-a-lees]
a group of mosquitoes of which the female carries the organism *Plasmodium* that causes malaria in humans.

antagonistic muscle pair
two muscles that work against each other at a joint. For example, the biceps contracts to bend the arm and the triceps contracts to straighten it.

antenna
1 feelers on the head of an insect or crustacean.
2 a wire used for sending or receiving electro-magnetic radiation. See **aerial.**

anther
the sac-like part of the stamen of a flower that produces the pollen. See **stamen, flower.**

antibiotic [an-ti-by-ot-ik]
a substance obtained from micro-organisms, especially moulds, that destroys or slows the growth of disease-causing bacteria and fungi. Penicillin, streptomycin and tetracycline are common antibiotics.

antibiotic resistance
overuse of antibiotics has led to the development of strains of bacteria that are resistant to the particular antibiotic.

antibody [an-ti-bod-i]
a protein made in the blood, as a defence against a substance (antigen) invading the body. A different antibody is made for each different antigen. Antibody molecules attach themselves to invading antigens and destroy them. See **antigen**.

antibody positive
the presence of a specific antibody in blood. This means that the organism has already been infected by the related antigen. See **HIV positive.**

anticlockwise
circular movement opposite in direction to the hands of a clock. ↺

antidote [an-ti-doht]
a substance that acts against the effects of a poison or a medicine that is causing harm.

antigen [an-ti-jen]
a substance that enters the body of an animal and causes the immune system to produce antibodies. The antibodies attack the antigens. Antigens may be dangerous infectious micro-organisms, material in the environment such as pollen dust, or even life-saving organ transplants. See **antibody**.

antiseptic
any substance that kills or stops the growth of disease-causing micro-organisms. See **disinfectant**.

anus [ay-nus]
the opening at the lower end of the alimentary canal (in most animals), through which solid waste is passed out. See **Fig. 1** (p. 5).

aorta [ay-or-ta]
the large artery that carries blood away from the left side of the heart. See **Fig. 19** (p. 67).

aperture
the opening in both the eye and the camera through which light enters. The pupil is the aperture of the eye. The size of the aperture can be controlled by the diaphragm. The iris is the diaphragm of the eye. See **diaphragm.**

aphid [ay-fid]
an insect that sucks juice from plants and can carry diseases.

apparatus
any object, instrument or machine used to carry out a

scientific experiment, e.g. a test tube, beaker, flask, funnel, thermometer.

appendix
small closed tube leading off from the intestine. The appendix has no part in digestion and absorption in humans. See **Fig. 1** (p. 5).

aquarium [a-kwair-i-um]
a container of water in which a variety of plants and animals are living.

aqueous humour
[**ay**-kwi-us **hew**-mer]
the watery liquid that fills the front part of the eye between the lens and the cornea.

aqueous solution
[**ay**-kwi-us]
a solution made by dissolving a substance in water.

aquifer [ak-wi-fer]
a layer of rock beneath the Earth's surface where useable water is trapped.

arachnid [a-**rak**-nid]
a member of the group of animals that includes spiders and scorpions.

arbitrary units [ar-bit-rer-i]
units made up of non-standard measurements such as a hand-span.

archaeology [ar-ki-**ol**-o-ji]
the study of the remains of the past.

area
the amount of surface. Measured in square metres (m^2), square centimetres (cm^2), square millimetres (mm^2), etc.

argon
symbol Ar. A colourless non-reactive gas element (Z=18). Used to fill electric light bulbs. See **noble gases.**

armature [ar-ma-choor]
the rotating coils in an electric motor or dynamo.

artery
thick-walled blood vessel that carries blood away from the heart to all parts of the body.

artesian water
[ar-tee-zhan]
water trapped between layers of rocks beneath the Earth's surface. The water is usually under pressure, and often gushes out at the surface when a well is drilled.

arthropod [arth-ro-pod]
an animal of the group that includes insects, spiders, crabs and centipedes. Arthropods have jointed legs and a hard covering (exoskeleton) over the body.

articulation
[ar-**tik**-yoo-lay-shn]
the joining of two bones usually by means of a joint.

artificial preservative
a chemical such as sodium nitrite NaNO$_2$ that destroys or prevents the growth of micro-organisms, and can be added to food to preserve it.

artificial satellite
a man-made object that orbits around the Earth, the Moon, the Sun or any other planet. Artificial satellites can take pictures, gather information from space and relay radio, TV and telephone signals from one part of the Earth to another.

artificial selection
breeding of animals and plants by mating parents chosen for particular characteristics. Farmers use artificial selection to produce better livestock.
See **natural selection**.

asbestos
a soft, fire-proof material. Once widely used as a building material, it was found to cause cancer and is now banned in many countries.

asexual reproduction
[ay-**seks**-yoo-al]
a form of reproduction in which a single parent produces offspring. The offspring are identical to the parent. Taking cuttings or growing, e.g. strawberry plants from 'runners', are examples of the use of asexual reproduction to produce new plants.
See **clone**.

aspirin
a substance used to relieve pain or fever.

assimilation
the use by a living organism of absorbed food chemicals in the process of growth, reproduction and repair.

asteroid [**ass**-ter-oid]
one of a group of small, rocky bodies usually found orbiting the Sun between Mars and Jupiter. The largest asteroid is over 900 km in diameter and the smallest less than 1 km.

astigmatism
[a-**stig**-ma-tism]
an eye problem caused by an irregularly shaped cornea. Reflected light from one point does not focus to a single point, causing a blurred image.

astrology [a-**strol**-o-ji]
the study of the movement of stars and planets based on the belief that these affect people's lives.
See **astronomy**.

astronaut
> a person who travels in a spacecraft.

astronomy [a-stron-o-mi]
> the scientific study of the stars and planets and their movement. Astronomy has revealed many of the physical laws that govern the universe.

atmosphere
> the layer of air that surrounds a planet. See **Earth's atmosphere.**

atmospheric corrosion
> a reaction between a metal and the oxygen and water in the air. Rusting is an example of atmospheric corrosion.

atmospheric pressure
> see **air pressure.**

atom
> the smallest particle of an element that can take part in a chemical reaction. It is made up of electrons orbiting a nucleus. All nuclei contain protons. All nuclei except hydrogen contain neutrons as well. See **atomic number, mass number.**

atomic bomb
> see **nuclear weapons.**

atomic energy
> see **nuclear energy.**

atomic mass
> the mass of an atom of an element as compared to the mass of an atom of carbon. A carbon atom is defined as having an atomic mass of 12. An atom of hydrogen has an atomic mass of 1 and an atom of oxygen has an atomic mass of 16.

atomic mass unit (amu)
> the unit used for measuring atomic masses. Defined as one twelfth of the mass of a neutral atom of the carbon-12 isotope (^{12}C).

atomic number
> symbol Z. The number of protons in the nucleus of an atom. All atoms of an element have the same atomic number.

atrium [ay-tri-um]
> a chamber in the upper part of the heart that receives blood from the veins and forces it, by muscular action, into a lower chamber called the ventricle. See **heart.**

attract
> to pull towards. Magnets attract iron. Positive charges attract negative charges.

attraction [a-trak-shn]
> a force pulling two objects together. See **repulsion.**

average
the value obtained by adding several quantities together and dividing by the number of quantities.

average speed
the total distance travelled, divided by the time it takes to travel that distance.

Aves [ay-vees]
the birds.

axillary bud [aks-il-er-i]
the growth bud in a plant that forms between the stem and each leaf.

axis
the imaginary line through the centre of a spinning object, e.g. the Earth turns on its axis once every 24 hours. See **Fig. 2**.

axle [ax-el]
a rod through the centre of a wheel, on which the wheel turns.

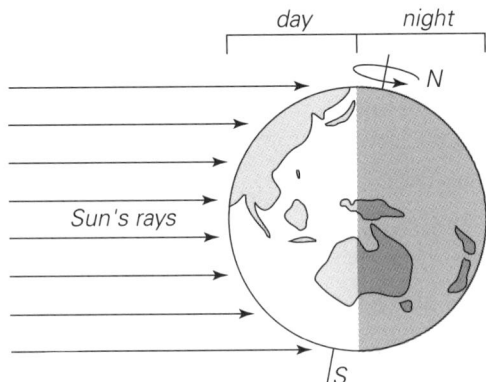

Fig. 2 the Earth turns on its axis. It completes one revolution in 24 hours. This causes day and night.

B

backbone
see **vertebral column**.

bacterium [bak-**teer**-ium]
(pl. bacteria) single-celled organism that is invisible to the naked eye, does not have a nuclear membrane. Some bacteria cause diseases in plants and animals.

balance
an accurate weighing machine. See **beam balance**, **spring balance**.

ball and socket joint
a joint between two bones that allows movement forwards, backwards and from side to side. The joint between the femur and the hip girdle (pelvis) is an example. See **Fig. 3**.

barometer [ba-**rom**-it-er]
an instrument for measuring atmospheric pressure. See **aneroid barometer**, **mercury barometer**.

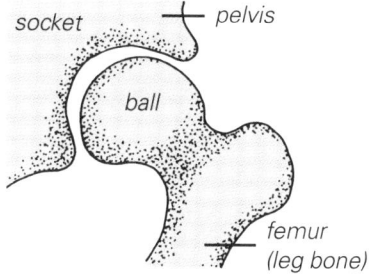

Fig. 3 ball and socket joint (hip)

basalt [ba-sawlt]
an igneous rock formed when lava cools quickly on the surface of the Earth.

base
a substance that can neutralise an acid. A base turns litmus blue and has a pH of more than 7. Bases include metal oxides, hydroxides, carbonates and ammonia.

basic

1. describing a compound that is a base.
2. describing an alkaline solution containing an excess of hydroxide OH$^-$ ions.

basic colours

the seven colours of the rainbow or visible spectrum: red, orange, yellow, green, blue, indigo and violet.

battery

two or more electrochemical cells connected together to form a source of electricity. A common car battery or accumulator usually consists of six electric cells in series. See **cell, primary cell, secondary cell**.

bauxite [bawk-syt]

a rock containing aluminium oxides from which aluminium is produced.

BCG vaccination

an important vaccination given to children to protect them from the disease tuberculosis (TB).

beam balance

a weighing device. The simplest beam balance consists of two pans suspended from a beam that is balanced at a central point. The object to be weighed is placed in one pan and known weights are added to the other pan.

bearings

ball bearings and roller bearings are used in many machines. They make surfaces roll rather than slide over one another, and therefore reduce friction.

bee

an insect that lives in a colony and is often kept for the honey it produces. Honeybee; *Apis mellifera*.

beetle

a type of insect with hard outer-wing covering.

beta particle [bee-ta]

sometimes written β-particle. A high-energy electron ejected from a nucleus during radioactive decay. As a result, the number of protons in the nucleus increases by one. See **nuclear radiation**.

beta radiation [bee-ta]

fast moving, high-energy electrons that can penetrate metal up to one centimetre thick. Can easily pass through skin and cause damage to cells. Also used to treat cancer.

biceps [by-seps]

the muscle that runs along the upper arm. It is

connected at one end to the radius and at the other to the shoulder bone (scapula). Contraction of the biceps causes the arm to bend at the elbow. See **antagonistic muscle pair**.

big-bang theory
the theory that the Universe and all matter and energy were created in the past as a huge explosion.

bile
a bitter-tasting greenish-yellow fluid, produced by the liver and stored in the gall bladder. It is secreted into the duodenum and used in the digestion of fats.

billion
usually one thousand million, 10^9. (Sometimes in the UK and Germany one million million, 10^{12}.)

bi-metallic strip
a device consisting of two different metal strips welded together. When heated, the bar bends because the different metals expand at different rates. Also called a compound bar.

binary code [**by**-ner-i]
the writing of all numbers using only two digits, 0 and 1. It is used in writing programs for computers and in the transmission of digital signals.

binary fission
see **fission**.

binocular vision [**byn**-ok-ew-ler **vi**-shn]
the ability of animals to use their eyes to produce three-dimensional images and therefore judge distance. The most successful animals have two forward-looking eyes at the front of the head.

binoculars [**byn**-ok-ew-lers]
any magnifying optical instrument that needs the use of both eyes.

biochemistry
[**by**-oh-**kem**-ist-ri]
the study of the chemistry of organisms.

biodegradable
describes materials that can be broken down (decomposed) by biological processes. See **pollution**.

biogas [**by**-oh gas]
gas produced by decaying organic matter. It is about 50% methane and can be used as a fuel for heating, cooking and lighting. See **alkane**.

biological control
the control of pests by biological means, e.g. the use of predators, rather than through the use of chemicals.

biology
the study of living things including their structure, function, origin, evolution, classification, interrelationships and distribution.

biomass
the total mass of all the organisms of a given type in an area, e.g. the biomass of all the trees in the Amazonian rain forest.

biosphere [by-o-sfeer]
the whole of the region of the Earth's surface including the sea, the land and the atmosphere, in which we find organisms.

biotechnology
[by-o tek-nol-o-ji]
the use of living organisms to make useful substances. See **fermentation, genetic engineering**. See also **Appendix 5**.

biotic factor
[by-**ot**-ik fak-tor]
any organism in the environment that may affect another organism. They may be competitors, predators, prey or pests.

bird
a warm-blooded animal that has feathers, a beak and wings and lays hard-shelled eggs that need incubating. Vertebrate of the class Aves.

birth control
avoiding pregnancy by natural or artificial means. See **condom, contraceptive, rhythm method**.

birth rate
the rate at which a population produces offspring, e.g. live births per 1000.

black hole
formed by the collapse of a very large star, a black hole has a gravitational field that is so strong that not even light can escape.

bladder
1 a hollow muscular organ in which urine is stored. Also called the urinary bladder. See **Fig. 14** (p. 53).
2 other sac-like storage organs in animals are also called bladders. See **gall bladder**.

blast furnace
a large furnace in which iron ore is heated with coke C and limestone $CaCO_3$ in a stream of air to produce iron.

blind spot
the spot on the retina at which all the blood vessels and nerve fibres enter the optic nerve. There are no rods and cones at this spot, therefore no image is recorded. See **Fig. 15** (p. 54).

blood

the liquid that circulates in the circulatory system of animals. It consists of blood cells and liquid plasma. Blood carries food, oxygen and hormones to all cells of the body. It carries carbon dioxide and waste products away from the cells. See **blood cell**, **haemoglobin**, **plasma**.

blood cell

any of the cells found in blood. See **erythrocyte**, **leucocyte**.

blood clotting

the process by which a plug of partly solid material is formed from blood platelets at e.g. a cut. Blood clotting helps stop bleeding and prevents bacteria entering the body.

blood plasma [plaz-muh]

pale yellow liquid—part of the blood that is left when the blood cells are removed. Consists of water containing dissolved substances including proteins, salts, sugars, hormones, vitamins and waste products.

blood platelets

very small cell fragments in the blood that are important in blood clotting.

blood poisoning

a condition in which the blood contains poisons such as those from an infection.

blood vessel

the tube-like structure through which the blood of an animal flows. See **artery**, **capillary**, **vein**.

boiling

the forming of many bubbles of vapour in a liquid, especially when it is being heated. The temperature of the liquid does not increase because energy is being used to turn the liquid into a gas. See **boiling point**.

boiling point

the temperature at which a liquid boils at atmospheric pressure.

bond

see **chemical bond**.

bond energy

the amount of energy stored in a chemical bond between two atoms in a compound.

botany

the study of plants.

brain

the enlarged top part of the central nervous system. The brain receives information from the sense organs and controls the muscles. The brain is protected by the skull.

braking distance
the distance travelled by a car from when the brakes are applied to when it stops.

brass
an alloy consisting of copper Cu and zinc Zn.

breathing
the process of taking air into the lungs (inhaling) and pushing air and waste gases out again (exhaling).

bromine [broh-meen]
symbol Br. A reactive element from Group 7 of the periodic table. It is a red, volatile liquid at room temperature.

bronchitis
[brong-**ky**-tiss]
infection of the walls of the bronchi. People who smoke are more likely to suffer from bronchitis.

bronchus [brong-kus]
the tube in the lungs that carries air (pl. bronchi). See **lung**.

bronze
an alloy of copper Cu and tin Sn, and sometimes lead Pb and zinc Zn.

budding
1 the process by which a single-celled plant, such as yeast, produces a new organism. It is an example of asexual reproduction. See **Fig. 4**.
2 a method of producing new plants in which a piece of bark containing a bud is removed from one plant and attached to another plant through a T-shaped cut in the bark.

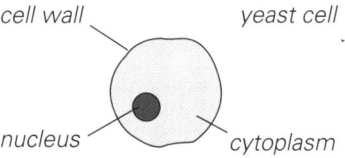
cell wall — yeast cell
nucleus — cytoplasm

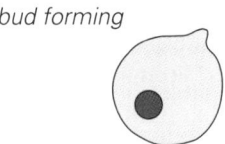
bud forming

growing bud

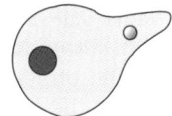
new daughter cell

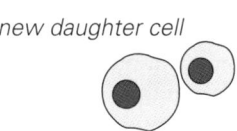

Fig. 4 budding in yeast

buffer solution
a solution that stops change of the pH of another solution, even if small amounts of acid or alkali are added.

Bunsen burner
a laboratory burner in which gas, usually natural gas (methane), is burnt with air. The temperature of the flame is controlled by a collar that can open or close an air hole. See **Fig. 5**.

by-product
a substance or material produced in the process of making something else.

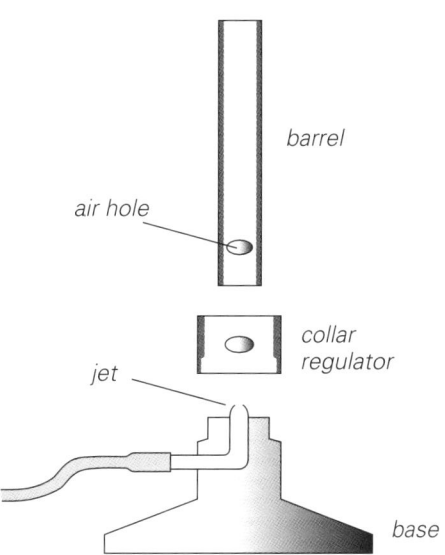

Fig. 5 construction of a Bunsen burner

calcium [kal-see-um]
symbol Ca. A soft, grey metal element in Group 2 of the periodic table. See **alkaline earth metals**.

calcium carbonate
[**kal**-see-um **kar**-bon-ayt] a white solid $CaCO_3$ that is found naturally as limestone, marble and coral. It is a base that is insoluble in water and reacts with acids to form a salt, carbon dioxide and water.

$$CaCO_3 + HCl \text{ (acid)} \downarrow$$
$$CaCl_2 + CO_2 + H_2O \text{ (salt)}$$

calcium hydroxide
[**kal**-see-um hy-**drok**-syd] a white solid $Ca(OH)_2$, that dissolves slightly in water. See **limewater, calcium oxide**.

calcium oxide
also known as lime or quicklime. A white solid CaO, formed by heating calcium carbonate.

$$CaCO_3 \rightarrow CaO + CO_2$$

Calcium oxide is an alkali and reacts with water to form calcium hydroxide and gives off much heat.

$$CaO + H_2O \rightarrow Ca(OH)_2 + \text{heat energy}$$

calibrate [kal-i-brayt]
to put the scale marks on a measuring instrument.

calorie
unit for measuring thermal energy (heat). The amount of heat needed to raise the temperature of one gram of water by one degree centigrade. Now replaced by the joule.

calyx [**kay**-liks]
the lower part of the flower that was the covering of the flower bud. The calyx is made up of several green leaf-like sepals.

cancer
a disease caused by the multiplication of an abnormal cell. The cells continue to multiply, forming a ball of cells called a tumour, which grows rapidly, invading and damaging vital organs. Smoking is a major cause of lung cancer. Ultraviolet light from the Sun can cause skin cancer.

canine [kay-nyn]
a cone-shaped tooth for piercing and tearing food.

capillary [ka-**pil**-er-i]
the smallest type of blood vessel. Capillaries take blood to all cells. Their walls are so thin that oxygen and dissolved food can pass through them to supply the cells. Capillaries receive blood from arteries and pass it on to veins.

capillary action
the process whereby a liquid rises up a narrow tube.

carbohydrate
[kar-bor-**hy**-drate]
solid substances made up from carbon, hydrogen and oxygen. They are the main source of energy for living things. Plants make carbohydrate sugars as a result of photosynthesis. Plants and animals make polymers of this sugar such as starch, cellulose and glycogen.
See **photosynthesis**.

carbon
symbol C. Non-metal element (Z=6). Carbon occurs in all organic compounds and is therefore the building block of all living things. Carbon has three main allotropic forms, including diamond and graphite. See **allotrope**.

carbon cycle
the movement of carbon between carbon dioxide in the atmosphere, living things and fossil fuels. Plants take in carbon dioxide during photosynthesis to form carbohydrates. Most living things give out carbon dioxide during respiration. See **Fig. 6** (p. 24).

carbon dating
estimating the age of the remains of organic material containing carbon, by measuring the amount of the radioactive isotope of carbon (carbon-14) remaining in the sample.

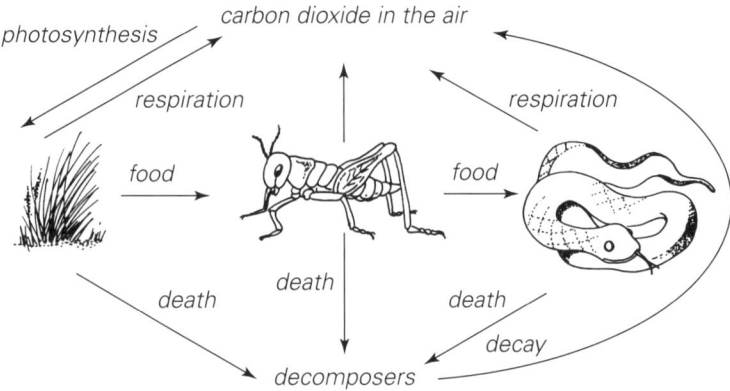

Fig. 6 the carbon cycle

carbon dioxide
a colourless, odourless gas CO_2 that is soluble in water. See **carbon cycle**.

carbon monoxide
a colourless and odourless but toxic gas CO. It is formed when carbon burns without enough oxygen. Many people die every year from carbon monoxide poisoning.

carcinogen [kar-sin-o-jen]
any substance that produces cancer, e.g. some of the chemicals in tobacco smoke and cigarette tar.

carnivore [kar-ni-vor]
a meat-eating animal. Carnivores usually have powerful jaws and canine teeth. See **consumer**.

carpel [kar-pel]
the complete female reproductive organ of a flower consisting of the stigma, style and ovary. See **flower** and **Fig. 16** (p. 57).

cartilage [kar-ti-lij]
a very strong and flexible tissue made of criss-crossed fibres. Cartilage is found on the end of bones in joints. The end of the nose also contains cartilage.

catalyst [kat-a-list]
a substance that speeds up a chemical reaction, without being changed or used during the reaction. See **enzyme**.

cathode [kath-ohd]
a negatively charged electrode. In a cell, the cathode releases electrons to

produce electricity. During electrolysis, the positively charged ions (cations) are attracted to the cathode. See **cation**, **cell**, **electrolysis**.

cation [kat-I-on]
an ion with a positive charge. Metal atoms lose electrons to form cations, e.g. sodium atoms lose one electron to form Na^+ cations, and calcium atoms lose two electrons to form Ca^{2+} cations. Cations are attracted to the cathode during electrolysis. See **cathode**, **cation**, **cell**, **electrolysis.**

caustic soda
see **sodium hydroxide**.

cell
1 a living cell is the smallest part of an organism. A cell is made up of protoplasm surrounded by a cell membrane. The protoplasm consists of a jelly-like protein, organelles and the nucleus. See **Fig. 7**.
2 a device that produces electricity. An electrochemical cell uses chemical reactions to produce a voltage. A solar cell uses sunlight to produce a voltage. See **battery**, **dry cell**, **lead-acid cell**, **primary cell**, **secondary cell**, **solar cell**.

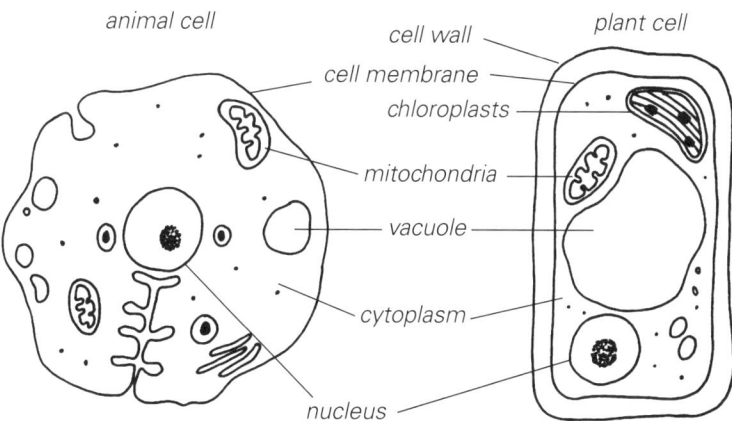

Fig. 7 typical animal and plant cells

cell body
the part of a neurone (nerve cell) that contains the nucleus. See **neurone**.

cell division
the formation of two or more cells from a single cell. The nucleus divides first, followed by the formation of cell membranes to divide the cell into new cells. See **mitosis**, **meiosis**.

cell membrane
the outer layer of a living cell that holds the cell together. The cell membrane controls the flow of substances into and out of the cell. See **Fig. 7** (p. 25).

cell wall
a rigid layer around the cell membrane of a plant and bacteria cell, which holds the cell together and gives it shape. The cell wall of plants contains cellulose. See **Fig. 7** (p. 25).

cellulose [sel-yoo-lohs]
a carbohydrate that makes up the cell walls of plants. Cellulose is a polymer of the sugar, glucose. Humans cannot digest cellulose. See **Ruminantia**.

Celsius scale [sel-si-us]
a scale for measuring temperature in degrees Celsius (°C). The two fixed points are the temperature of ice in water 0°C, and the temperature of steam above boiling water 100°C.

cement
1 bony material that holds a tooth in the jawbone.
2 a grey powder made by roasting and crushing a mixture of limestone and clay. It sets as a hard mass when mixed with water.

centigrade scale
[sent-i-grayd]
the old name for the Celsius scale for measuring temperature.

central nervous system
in vertebrates, the part of the nervous system consisting of the brain and the spinal cord.

central processing unit
the part of a computer that processes the data. It is also known as the CPU.

centripetal force
[sen-**trip**-i-tal]
the force, acting towards the centre, that makes a body travel in a circular path. The gravitational force of the Sun is the centripetal force that keeps planets orbiting the Sun.

cerebrum [se-ri-brum]
the largest region of the brain. It is the region from

which thought, memory and movement are controlled, and where information from the sense organs is received.

cervix [ser-viks]
the narrow neck of the uterus where it connects to the top of the vagina in female mammals.

CFC [see ef see]
chlorofluorocarbon. Used in some aerosols and in refrigeration systems. In the atmosphere, CFCs break down ozone. Their use has been banned in many countries. See **ozone layer**.

chain reaction
a reaction in which the products cause the reaction to continue. The nuclear fission of a uranium-235 atom produces three neutrons that cause the fission of three more uranium-235 atoms, and so on.

change of state
the process by which matter changes from one state to another. See **states of matter, boiling, freezing, evaporation, condensation, melting, sublimation**.

charcoal
a form of carbon produced by heating organic matter. Charcoal from wood is used as a fuel.

charge
a property of some particles. A proton has a positive charge and an electron has a negative charge. Particles with an opposite charge attract one another, and those with the same charge repel each other.

chemical
a single pure substance that is either an element or a compound.

chemical bond
a strong force of attraction that holds atoms together in a compound. Energy is released when a chemical bond is broken. See **ionic bond, covalent bond**.

chemical change
see **chemical reaction**.

chemical energy
the energy in the chemical bonds of a substance.

chemical equation
the formulae, and number of molecules or atoms of reactants and products, that take part in a chemical reaction. The reactants are to the left of the equation and the products to the right. The arrow shows the direction of the chemical change.

$CaCO_3 \longrightarrow CaO + CO_2$
(reactant)   (products)

chemical formula
the symbol showing the number and type of atoms that make up a compound, e.g. sodium chloride = NaCl, water = H_2O.

chemical reaction
a chemical change in which one or more elements or compounds (reactants) change to form new elements or compounds (products).

chemical symbol
an abbreviation for the name of an element. Chemical symbols are used for writing formulae for compounds, and for chemical equations. Many symbols are abbreviations of the Latin name for the element, e.g. the symbol for iron is Fe, from the Latin word for iron, *ferrum*. See **Appendix 2**.

chemistry
the study of elements and their compounds.

chlorine [klor-een]
symbol Cl. A non-metallic element of Group 7 of the periodic table (Z=17). It is a poisonous, greenish-yellow gas at room temperature.

chlorophyll [klo-ro-fil]
the green pigment in plants that absorbs the light energy from the Sun. It is stored as chemical energy in the glucose molecules produced during photosynthesis. A molecule of chlorophyll contains magnesium atoms and is related chemically to haemoglobin.
See **photosynthesis**.

chloroplast [klo-ro-plast]
lens-shaped microscopic organs inside plant cells that contain chlorophyll. Photosynthesis takes place inside the chloroplast. See **Fig. 7** (p. 25).
See **photosynthesis.**

chromatography
[kroh-ma-**tog**-raf-i]
a method for separating coloured substances in a mixture. A solvent is used to move the substances across an absorbent surface.

chromosome
[kroh-mo-sohm]
a thread-like structure found in pairs in the nucleus of plant and animal cells. One chromosome of each pair is inherited from each parent. Chromosomes contain genes that, in pairs, control the inherited characteristics of an organism.

chromosphere
[kroh-mos-feer]
the layer of the Sun's atmosphere surrounding the photosphere. The chromosphere can be seen during a total eclipse. See **photosphere.**

cilium [sil-i-um]
a hair-like thread that grows from some cells (pl. cilia). Some microbes use cilia for movement. In larger animals, cilia are used to move fluids, e.g. the cells lining the trachea and bronchi.

circuit [ser-kit]
a complete path made from electrical conductors through which electricity can flow. See **parallel circuit, series circuit**.

circuit breaker
an electromagnetic safety switch that breaks an electrical circuit if the current is too high. See **fuse**.

circulatory system [ser-kew-**layt**-eri]
the heart, blood vessels, blood, lymphatic vessels and lymph that together, in animals, carry food and waste products to and from all cells. The heart is the pump for the circulatory system.

classification
a method for sorting living things into different groups. Each group consists of organisms with similar characteristics. The simplest classification places all living things into two groups: animals and plants.

climate
the weather conditions of a location as described for a whole year. Rainfall, temperature, winds and hours of sunshine are some of the properties used to describe climate.

climax community
the stable biological community that is the end product of biological succession. See **succession**.

clinical thermometer
a thermometer used to measure the temperature of humans.

clitoris [klit-er-iss]
the small rod of sensitive tissue found at the front of the vagina of female mammals and some birds and reptiles.

clone [klo-n]
a plant or animal that is genetically identical to its parent. Clones are produced naturally by asexual reproduction, e.g. splitting of one amoeba into two.

clotting
see **blood clotting**.

cloud
a mass of water droplets or ice crystals held in suspension in the atmosphere. Clouds are formed by the condensation of water vapour around dust or

smoke particles. See **condensation**.

coal
a solid, black fossil fuel formed from plants that grew over 200 million years ago. Coal is mainly composed of carbon.

coelenterate
[see-**len**-ter-ayt]
a group of invertebrate animals that have a soft bag-shaped body with one opening. Coelenterates have tentacles with stinging cells. Examples include jellyfish and sea anemones. See **nematocyst**.

coke
a form of carbon made from coal. It is used as a fuel and in making iron. See **blast furnace**.

cold-blooded
animals whose internal body temperature is the same as that of their environment. Cold-blooded animals include insects, reptiles, fish and amphibians but not birds and mammals. See **poikilotherm**.

colon [koh-lon]
the main part of the large intestine before the rectum. Water and mineral salts are absorbed into the body by the colon. See **Fig. 1** (p. 5).

colony
1 a group of microbes such as yeast or bacteria that have developed from one parent cell.
2 a group of animals of the same species that live together. Coral consists of a colony of animals that are physically joined together, whereas insects such as bees are not physically joined but are highly organised.

colour
the sensation produced when light of different wavelengths fall on the human eye. See **primary colour**, **secondary colour**.

colour blindness
an inherited problem affecting eyes, suffered more by men than women. People with colour blindness cannot tell some colours apart.

combustion
[kom-**bus**-chn]
burning; a chemical reaction that takes place between a substance and oxygen. Energy is released during the reaction, in the form of heat and light.
See **exothermic**.

comet
a small celestial body made up of dust, ice and gas, that travels around the Sun. Comets can be seen when

they are nearest the Sun. Solar winds cause comets to have a tail that always points away from the Sun. See **solar system**.

communication
the process whereby a message is sent by one person and understood by another person.

communication satellite
a geostationary satellite used for broadcasting television and telephone communications between different parts of the world. See **geostationary satellite**.

community
a group of organisms living together in a habitat. They have an effect on each other and are linked together in a food web. See **succession**, **ecosystem**.

commutator
[**kom**-yoo-tay-ter]
the ends of the wire coil that spins around in an electric motor or generator through which connections are made to the external circuit. Carbon brushes press against the commutator and carry current into or away from the spinning coil.

compact disk
a disk (CD) on which digital information, e.g. music or computer data, is stored on a reflective metal layer as tiny pits on a spiral track. The information is read by a low-energy laser focused on the track.

compass
an instrument, used for navigation, consisting of a small magnet balanced at its centre. The magnet aligns itself in the Earth's magnetic field so that its north-seeking pole points north.

competitor
any organism that competes for food or living space with other organisms.

complementary colours
two coloured lights that produce white light when combined, e.g. yellow and blue.

compost
plant material that is collected and allowed to decay. Compost is used to increase the humus content of soils.

compound [**kom**-pownd]
a substance that contains two or more elements joined together by chemical bonds. See **covalent compound**, **ionic compound**, **organic compound**.

compound bar
see **bi-metallic strip**.

compound eye
the eye of insects and crustaceans that is made up of thousands of tiny eye units.

compression
[kom-**pre**-shn]
a pushing force that causes something to squash. Compression of a gas decreases its volume and increases its pressure. See **tension**.

computer
an electrical device that takes in, stores and processes data to solve problems. Data is taken in from a keyboard, a disk or tape, or from another computer. The data is processed by the central processing unit (CPU) using a program.

concave
curving inwards. A concave lens (divergent lens) has one or both surfaces curved inwards. A concave lens spreads out (diverges) a beam of light as if it comes from one point. Images formed by concave lenses are smaller than the object and the same way up. A concave mirror has a reflecting surface that is curved inwards. See **Fig. 8**.

concave lens or mirror
see **concave**.

concentrated solution
a solution that contains a large amount of a dissolved substance.

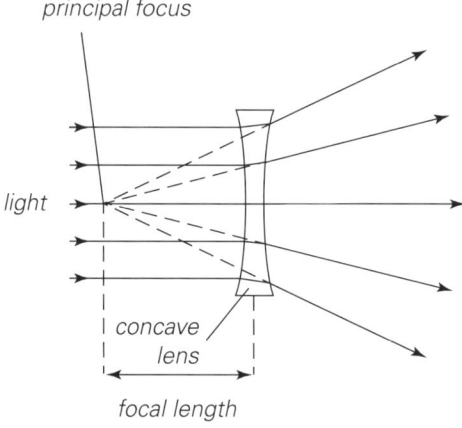

Fig. 8 concave lens

concentration
the amount of solute dissolved in a certain volume of solvent, e.g. if 20 grams of salt is dissolved in 200 cm^3 of water, the solution has a concentration of 100 grams per litre (100g/dm^3).

conception [kon-**sep**-shn]
the fertilization in the Fallopian tubes of a mammalian egg cell by a sperm cell.

conclusion [kon-**klu**-shn]
a statement at the end of an experiment of what you have found out.

condensation
[**kon**-den-**say**-shn]
the process whereby a gas or vapour changes back to a liquid. Condensation is the opposite of evaporation and boiling. During condensation, heat (thermal) energy is released.

condensation polymerization
see **polymer**.

condenser
a device used to cool a vapour and change it into a liquid. A Liebig condenser consists of a glass pipe through which a vapour passes, surrounded by another pipe through which cold water flows. See **distillation**.

condom
a thin rubber sheath that fits over the penis before sexual intercourse to prevent pregnancy. Condoms reduce the risk of some sexually transmitted diseases. See **contraceptive**, **safer sex**.

conduction
1 thermal conduction is the movement of heat energy through a substance. When a substance is heated, the particles take in energy and vibrate and move faster. In solids such as metals that are good conductors of heat, electrons move freely between atoms and carry the heat energy to all parts. In liquids and gases, the heat is conducted by the movement of the atoms and molecules themselves.
2 electrical conduction is the passage of electricity through a substance. Metals and the non-metal graphite are good conductors of electrical energy. Electrons move freely between atoms, carrying the electrical energy (electric current) from one end of the circuit to the other.

conductivity
[kon-**dukt**-i-vi-ti]
a measure of how easily heat (thermal energy) or an electric current can pass through a substance. See **conduction**, **conductor**, **insulators**.

conductor
a substance through which heat (thermal energy) or electricity can easily flow. Metals and the non-metal graphite are good conductors because they have electrons that are free to move and carry energy from one place to another.

cone cell
a light sensitive cell in the retina of the eye. Cone cells work best in bright light and are responsible for colour vision.

conglomerate
[kon-**glom**-er-ayt]
a sedimentary rock made up of pebbles or gravel cemented together.

conifers
plants, including pines, that have seeds contained in cones. Seed bearing plants of the family *Coniferophyta*.

conservation
the careful use of natural resources, including a slowing down of the use of non-renewable resources; development of renewable alternatives; recycling; reduction of pollution and caring for nature.

conservation of energy
a law stating that energy is neither created nor destroyed but rather changes from one form to another, e.g. the total energy, including light and heat energy, given out by a light bulb is equal to the electrical energy used.

conservation of mass
a law that states that the total mass of the reactants at the beginning of a chemical reaction is equal to the total mass of products at the end of the reaction. (This law does not apply to nuclear reactions.)

conservation of momentum
a law that states that in a collision between objects, the total momentum does not change. Momentum cannot be created or destroyed.

constellation
[**khon**-ster-**lay**-shn]
a group of stars that seem, from the Earth, to form a recognisable shape, e.g. the constellation that the ancient Greeks named *Ursa Major* (Great Bear) is now thought to look like a plough or a giant ladle ('big dipper').

consumer
an organism that obtains its food by eating plants and animals. Primary consumers that eat plants are called herbivores. Carnivores that eat herbivores are called secondary consumers. Tertiary consumers are carnivores that feed on other carnivores.

contact metamorphism
[met-a-**morf**-izm] changes in rocks that result from coming into contact with hot magma. See **metamorphic rocks**.

continental drift
the gradual movement of the Earth's geological plates causing continents to move apart. See **plate tectonics**.

contraception
see **birth control**.

contraceptive
[**kon**-tra-**sep**-tiv] something that prevents sexual intercourse from resulting in pregnancy. Common contraceptives include condoms, diaphragms and pills. A condom is a thin rubber cover worn over the penis to catch the sperm. A diaphragm covers a woman's cervix, stopping sperm coming into contact with ova. The contraceptive pill contains hormones that stop ovulation.

contract [kon-**trakt**]
to become shorter in length. For example, metals contract when they are cooled.

contraction
[kon-**trak**-shn] the shortening of an object or a muscle. The word contraction is also used to describe the repeated contractions of the wall of the mother's uterus during birth.

control
part of an experiment that is used for purposes of comparison, e.g. when testing the effect of a fertilizer on plant growth, a control will have the same type of plants growing under exactly the same conditions but with no fertilizer.

convection
the movement of heat through liquids and gases, caused by the movement of the liquid or the gas itself.

convection current
the natural movement of warm air in the atmosphere or warm water in the oceans.

convex
curving outwards. A convex lens (convergent lens) has one or both surfaces curved outwards. A convex lens

brings together (converges) a beam of light to one point. Images formed by convex lenses are larger than the object and upside down. A convex mirror has a reflecting surface that is curved outwards. See **Fig. 9**.

convex lens or mirror
see **convex**.

cooling
loss of heat (thermal) energy resulting in a drop in temperature.

copper
symbol Cu. A red-brown, metallic element (Z= 29). It is an element that humans have extracted and used for thousands of years. It is an excellent conductor of heat and electricity and can be drawn into thin wires.

core
1 a piece of iron used to increase the strength of the magnetic field in an electric motor, transformer or electromagnet.
2 the central region of a planet or a star.
3 the inner part of a nuclear reactor.

cornea [kor-ni-a]
the transparent tissue that forms the front part of the eye over the lens and iris. See **Fig. 15** (p. 54).

corrosion
chemical reactions that take place attacking the surface of metals. Corrosion is usually caused by water and oxygen in the air. See **rusting**.

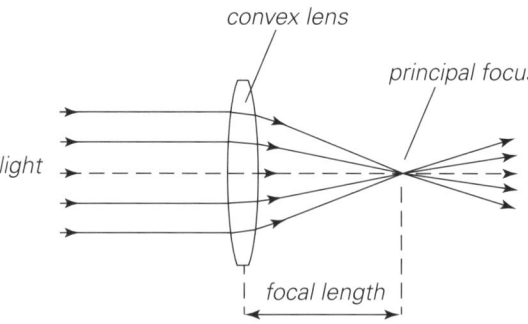

Fig. 9 convex lens

cotyledon [kot-i-lee-**don**]
a leaf that is part of the embryo plant inside a seed. Seeds have one or two cotyledons, which are a store of food used for the early growth of the plant.

covalent bond
[koh-**vay**-lent]
a force of attraction between two atoms resulting from their sharing a pair of electrons, e.g. a molecule of water is held together because there is a covalent bond between the atom of oxygen and each of the two atoms of hydrogen.

covalent compound
[koh-**vay**-lent]
a compound formed from non-metal atoms held together by covalent bonds, e.g. CO_2. Covalent compounds have low melting and boiling points and do not conduct electricity when melted.

cracking
a process in which large hydrocarbon molecules are broken down into smaller molecules. The process is called catalytic cracking when a catalyst is used. See **catalyst**.

crater
a bowl-shaped depression found, e.g. on the Moon caused by meteor impact, and at the top of volcanoes.

crescent
the curved shape of the Moon in its first and last quarter. See **phases of the Moon**.

crude oil
also called petroleum. A dark, liquid fuel formed from plant material that is over 250 million years old. It is a mixture of more that 300 different hydrocarbons.

crust
the outer part of the Earth that covers the mantle. Under the continents, the crust is up to 70 km thick, and under oceans, only 8 km thick.

crustacean [krus-**tay**-shn]
a type of arthropod animal including prawns, crabs and lobsters.

crystal
a solid with regular shapes and straight edges. Crystals are formed by evaporating solutions or cooling molten substances till they solidify.

crystallization
the process in which crystals form from a solution as it cools or evaporates.

current
see **electric current**.

cycle
a regularly repeated series of changes that brings things back to where they started. See **carbon cycle**.

cyclone [sy-klohn]
an area of low-pressure air in the atmosphere, also known as a depression. The pressure is lowest in the centre and strong winds circle towards the centre, usually bringing rain. See **Fig. 10**.

cytoplasm [sy-to-plazm]
the jelly-like contents of a living cell, not including the nucleus. The cytoplasm consists of water, salts, dissolved organic compounds such as glucose, and amino acids and organelles. See **Fig. 7** (p. 25).

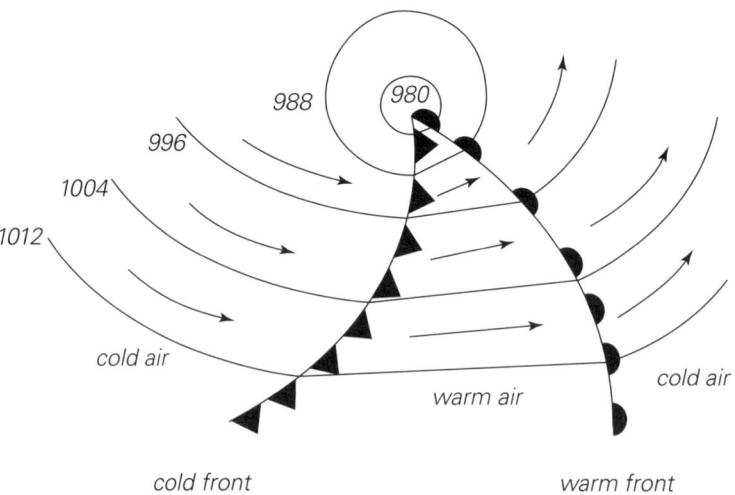

Fig. 10 a cyclone or depression as it appears on a weather map. The numbers indicate atmospheric pressure in millibars.

Darwinism
a theory of evolution advanced by Charles Darwin in 1859 after a visit to the Pacific region. He suggested that all species change over time. Those individuals best suited to the environment have a better chance to survive and multiply and therefore pass on their characteristics to the next generation. He called this 'natural selection'. He argued that these changes lead, over a long period of time, to new species.
See **evolution**, **natural selection**.

data
a collection of information. Computers use and store data expressed in binary code. See **binary code**.

database
information about a particular subject that has been classified and stored in a computer in such a way that it can be extracted under different headings.

d.c.
the abbreviation for direct current. See **electric current**.

death
the point at which the processes that maintain a living organism stop functioning.

death rate
the rate at which a particular species or population dies, e.g. deaths per 1000.
Compare **birth rate**.

decay
1 the decomposing of dead animal and plant material.
2 the breaking down of a radioactive nucleus into smaller particles. The time taken for half the radioactive nuclei to decay is called the half-life of the element.

decay organism
see **decomposer**.

decibel [dess-i-bel]
a unit used for the loudness of sounds.

deciduous [de-**sid**-yoo-us]
a plant that loses all its leaves at the beginning of the dry season in the tropics, or before winter in cold climates. This helps to conserve water that would normally be lost by evaporation through the leaves.

decomposer
an animal or plant that can break down dead organisms into simple substances. See **saprophyte**.

decomposition
the chemical breaking down of organic material into simpler chemicals by decomposers.

defecation [def-i-kay-shn]
the expulsion of faeces from the body through the anus. See **faeces**.

deforestation
the cutting down and clearing of forests. Deforestation causes soil erosion and may contribute to global warming.

degree
symbol °.
1 a unit for measuring angles. There are 360° in a circle.
2 a unit for measuring temperature. See **Celsius Scale**.

dehydration
the removal of water from a substance.

demagnetize
to treat a permanent magnet so that it loses its magnetism.

denitrifying bacteria
[dee-**ny**-tri-fy-ing bak-**teer**-ri-a]
bacteria that can turn nitrates and ammonia into nitrogen gas.

density
the mass of one cubic metre of a substance. Density is calculated by the formula:

$$\text{density} = \frac{\text{mass}}{\text{volume}}$$

deoxygenated blood
see **haemoglobin**.

deposition
the depositing of material. Sediments carried by rivers are deposited on the sea bed. During electrolysis, metal from the electrolyte can be deposited on the cathode. See **electroplating**.

dermis
the inner layers of the skin. See **skin** and **Fig. 39** (p. 130).

desalination [**dee**-sal-i-**nay**-shn]
the removal of salt from seawater so that the water can be used for irrigation or human consumption.

deuterium [dew-**teer**-i-um]
a heavy isotope of hydrogen where each atom contains one proton and one neutron in its nucleus. The nucleus of a 'normal' hydrogen atom contains one proton but no neutron.

development
in biology, the complex changes that take place as a single cell divides and multiplies to become an organism.

device
a tool or piece of equipment that has been designed for a special purpose.

dew
see **precipitation**.

dew point
the temperature at which air is saturated with water vapour. If the temperature falls below the dew point, the vapour condenses as drops of water.

diabetes [dy-a-**bee**-teez]
a disease caused by the pancreas producing too little of the hormone insulin. Sugar levels in the blood become dangerously high. Diabetes can be controlled by diet and by the regular injection of insulin.

diamond
a crystalline allotrope of pure carbon. It is the hardest known mineral and is used in grinding and cutting tools. Diamonds are transparent with a high refractive index. This makes them sparkle and so they are used in jewellery.

diaphragm [**dy**-a-fram]
1 a device used to control the amount of light entering a camera, a microscope or the eye. The iris is the diaphragm of the eye.
2 a muscular sheet at the base of the ribs that separates the thorax (chest) from the abdomen. The contraction and relaxation of the diaphragm helps the movement of air in and out of the lungs during breathing.

diatom [**dy**-a-tom]
marine and fresh water, single-celled algae that have

diatomic gas [dy-a-**tom**-ik] gas whose molecules contain two atoms joined by covalent bonds. Oxygen O_2, hydrogen H_2, chlorine Cl_2 and carbon monoxide CO are diatomic gases.

silica-containing, glass-like cell walls. They are found in huge numbers and are an important part of the food chain. Deposits of diatoms from the past have resulted in oil deposits.

dicotyledon [dy-kot-i-**lee**-don] one of a large group of plants whose seeds have two seed leaves (cotyledons).

diffusion [di-**few**-shn] the movement of a substance, usually a gas or a dissolved solute, from a region of high concentration to a region of low concentration. See **passive transport**, **active transport**.

digestion the process of breaking down complex food substances into simple molecules that can be absorbed into the organism. It takes place with the help of enzymes in the alimentary canal.

digit a single number (numeral). There are ten digits in the decimal counting system: 0, 1, 2, 3, 4, 5, 6, 7, 8, 9. There are two digits in the binary system: 0, 1. See **binary code**.

digital information coded as a series of numbers, usually in binary code. Computers use binary numbers to store and manipulate data. Audio and video signals can be transmitted digitally.

dilate [**dy**-late] to expand or get wider. For example, the eye pupil dilates when the intensity of light decreases.

dilute a solution that contains only a small amount of dissolved substance (solute).

diode [**dy**-ode] an electronic component that allows current to flow in one direction only.

direct current an electric current that flows only in one direction. See **d.c.**, **electric current**.

disinfectant a chemical substance that kills or stops the growth of disease-causing bacteria.

disk a thin sheet of magnetic material used to store digital computer information, including data and programs. Information can be read from the disk or written onto the disk by the computer. (Sometimes spelt **disc**.)

dispersal
the process that spreads seeds away from the parent plant. Seeds are dispersed by wind, water and animals.

dispersion
the separation of white light into a spectrum of colours, e.g. by a prism or a raindrop. See **refraction**.

displacement reaction
a reaction in which a more reactive metal takes the place of a less reactive metal in a compound. For example, magnesium will displace copper from copper(II) sulphate solution.

distillation
a process used to separate a liquid from a solution, e.g. pure water from sea water. The solution is heated, the liquid boils and turns to vapour. The vapour is cooled and condenses to form the pure liquid. See **Fig. 11**.

distilled water
water purified by distillation.

diverging lens or mirror
see **concave**.

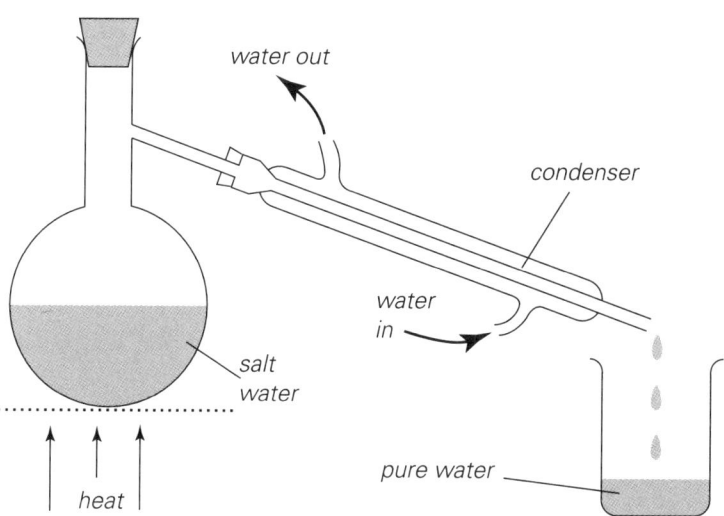

Fig. 11 *distillation of salt water*

DNA

DNA controls the way an organism develops, by controlling the manufacture of proteins. It is a nucleic acid (deoxyribonucleic acid) found in the chromosomes that make up the genes.

dominant gene

pairs of genes, one on each of a pair of chromosomes, control an organism's characteristics. Sometimes a characteristic is controlled by one of the genes, which 'overpowers' the effect of its partner. This is a **dominant** gene. The other gene is called a **recessive** gene, e.g. the gene for brown eyes is dominant over the gene for blue eyes.
See **allele**.

donor

1. an atom, ion or molecule that provides a pair of electrons for sharing with another atom, to form a covalent chemical bond.
2. an individual who provides an organ for transplanting in another individual. Donors also provide blood for transfusion.

dormancy

an inactive period in the life of a plant or an animal during which growth slows or completely stops. See **hibernation, deciduous**.

dosimeter

a device used to measure the amount of radiation absorbed.

drought [*rhymes with* out]

a long period with no rain.

drug

a chemical substance that changes the normal working of an organism. Drugs are used for the prevention and treatment of disease. Some drugs, such as alcohol, are used for recreation but can be dangerous and habit-forming.

dry cell

an electrochemical cell in which the electrolyte is a paste and not a liquid. The batteries used to power radios, calculators and torches are dry cells. Most dry cells are primary cells and cannot be recharged. See **electrochemical cell, primary cell, secondary cell**.

duodenum

[dew-o-**deen**-um]
the first section of the small intestine immediately after the stomach. Small glands in the wall of the duodenum secrete digestive enzymes. Bile from the gall bladder and other digestive enzymes from the pancreas are also secreted into the duodenum. See **Fig. 1** (p. 5).

eardrum [ear drum]
the thin sheet of skin that vibrates when sound waves enter the ear.

Earth
the third planet in the solar system, having an orbit between Venus and Mars. It has an atmosphere of 78% nitrogen, 21% oxygen, with small amounts of carbon dioxide and noble (inert) gases. The Moon is the only natural satellite of the Earth. See **Appendix 4**.

earthing
the connection of an object to the huge mass of the Earth through a conductor. This safety device allows charges to flow away, preventing shocks to humans and damage, e.g. to buildings. A lightning conductor is an example of earthing.

earthquake
a sudden movement in the Earth's crust and the resulting shock waves. They are the result of pressure building up between the Earth's tectonic plates and then being released. See **plate tectonics**.

Earth's atmosphere
the gas that surrounds the Earth. The composition is approximately 78% nitrogen, 21% oxygen and small amounts of carbon dioxide and noble (inert) gases. Air also contains varying amounts of water vapour. The atmosphere has various layers, beginning with the lowest level, the troposphere, where weather occurs. See **stratosphere**, **ionosphere**.

echo
the reflection of a wave from a surface, e.g. sound waves echo off a surface to return to the source as a weaker sound.

echo sounder
an instrument using reflected sound or ultrasound to measure the depth of water under a ship.

eclipse
an eclipse of the Sun (solar eclipse) takes place when the shadow of the Moon falls on the Earth. An eclipse of the Moon (lunar eclipse) takes place when the Sun, Earth and Moon are in a straight line and the shadow of the Earth falls on the Moon. See **Fig. 12**.

ecology [ee-**kol**-o-ji]
the study of how living things depend on each other and the natural environment they live in. See **habitat, ecosystem, environment, community**.

ecosystem [eek-oh-sis-tem]
a community of organisms, including their physical surroundings. The organisms in an ecosystem consist of green plants (producers) that are eaten by

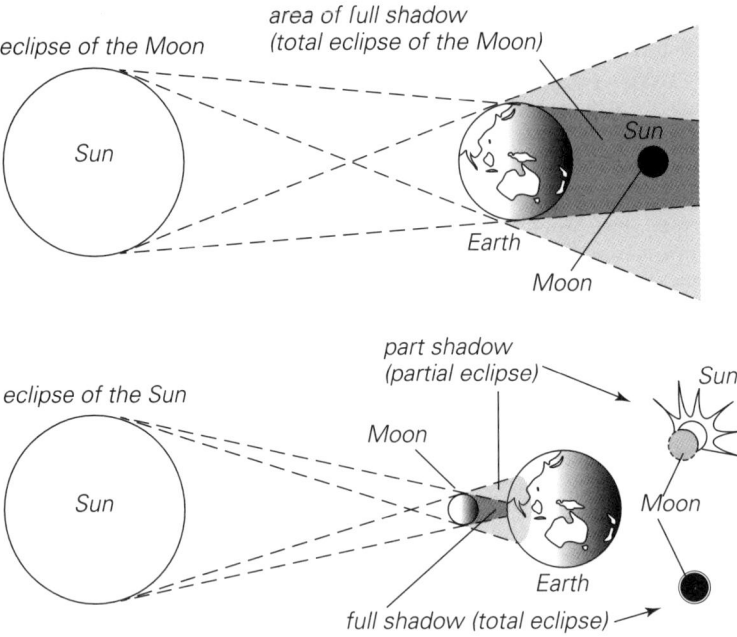

Fig. 12 eclipse of the Sun and eclipse of the Moon

herbivores (primary consumers), herbivores that are eaten by carnivores (secondary consumers), and decomposers that break down dead organisms and return nutrients to the soil.

efficiency
[**ee**-fish-n-see]
a measure of how well a machine changes energy into useful work. It is measured in percent, e.g. a petrol engine is 15% efficient. For every 100 joules of energy contained in the fuel used, 15 joules of useful work is done. The other 85 joules are lost as heat and noise.

effort
the force given to a machine to move a load. See **Fig. 34** (p. 115).

egestion [ee-jest-yn]
the expelling of unused and waste materials from the body. See **defecation**, **excretion**, **ingestion**.

egg
another word for ovum, in particular an ovum that has come from the body of an egg-laying animal. The eggs of birds, reptiles and insects have hard shells and consist of a fertilised ovum and a source of food (yoke). Eggs of fish and Amphibia have no hard shell and are fertilised after they are laid in water.

ejaculation
[e-**jak**-yoo-lay-shn]
the release of semen from the male penis during sexual intercourse. It is the peak of sexual excitement. See **orgasm**.

elasticity [e-las-tis-ity]
the tendency of a material to return to its original size and shape after it has been stretched, compressed or twisted.

electric charge
see **charge**.

electric current
a movement of electric charge. When a battery is connected in a circuit, electrons flow from the battery through the circuit, through the bulb and back to the battery. Before the discovery of the electron, scientists said that electric current flowed from the positive terminal of the battery, through the circuit to the negative terminal. This is still called the conventional current. We now know that current is a flow of electrons from the negative terminal of the battery through the circuit to the positive terminal. The electric current flowing through an electrolyte is a

flow of charged ions. See **alternating current**, **direct current**.

electric motor
a machine that converts electrical energy into movement (kinetic) energy. It consists of a fixed magnet and a coil that is free to rotate. Electric current passes through the coil, converting it into an electromagnet. The forces between the fixed magnet and the electromagnet coil cause the coil to rotate.

electrical energy
the energy of the electric charges (electrons) as they flow as a current through a circuit.

electrochemical cell
a cell that uses chemical reactions to produce an electric current. The cell consists of an electrolyte in contact with two electrodes. Chemical reactions between the electrodes and the electrolyte produce the electric current. See **cell**, **primary cell**, **secondary cell**.

electrode [e-**lek**-trohd]
an electrical conductor that either collects or gives off electrons. Cells and other electrical components have electrodes. In an electric cell, the negative electrode produces electrons and is called the cathode. The positive electrode to which electrons flow, is called the anode. In electrolysis, two electrodes are submerged in an electrolyte and are connected to a battery. See **anode**, **cathode**, **cell**, **electrolysis**.

electrolysis [e-lek-**trol**-i-sis]
a chemical reaction caused by passing electricity through an electrolyte. Two electrodes are submerged in an electrolyte and connected to a battery. See **anode**, **cathode**, **electrode**, **electrolyte**, **electroplating**.

electrolyte [e-**lek**-tro-lyt]
a liquid that contains ions and conducts electricity. Solutions of ionic substances, or melted (molten) ionic substances, are electrolytes. See **electrode**, **electrolysis**.

electromagnet
a temporary magnet made up of a coil of wire wound round a piece of iron. When electricity is passing through the coil of wire, the piece of iron becomes magnetized. When no current flows through the coil, the iron is not magnetized.

electromagnetic energy
the energy contained in electromagnetic radiation such as light, X-rays, radio

waves and gamma radiation. The higher the frequency of the radiation, the greater the energy.

electromagnetic radiation

energy that travels at the speed of light. Light, X-rays, radio waves and gamma radiation are examples. Electromagnetic radiation can be thought of as either a wave of energy, or as a stream of energy particles (photons).

electromagnetic spectrum

the full range of electromagnetic radiation listed in order of wavelength. The longest are radio waves followed by infra-red, visible light, ultraviolet, X-rays and gamma rays.

electromotive force

a measure of the amount of energy given to charged particles by a battery or a generator. It is measured in volts. See **potential difference**.

electron

a particle found in all atoms and ions except a positively charged hydrogen H^+ ion. An electron has a negative charge (–) equal and opposite to the positive charge (+) on a proton. An electron is 1/1840 of the mass of a proton.

electron shell

electrons orbit around the nucleus of an atom in groups. These groups are called shells. The nearest group of electrons to the nucleus is called the K shell and can contain a maximum of two electrons. The next shell is the L shell and can contain up to 8 electrons. The outer shell of an atom can lose or gain electrons to form ions. Atoms can also share outer shell electrons with other atoms to form covalent bonds. See **Fig. 13**.

electronics

the study and use of circuits that use electronic components such as transistors and 'microchips'.

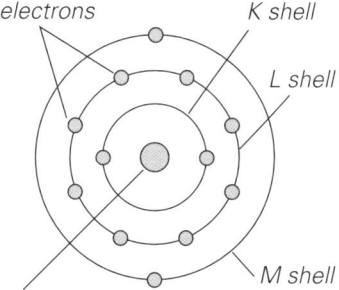

Fig. 13 arrangement of the twelve electrons around the nucleus of a magnesium atom

electroplating
using electrolysis to cover one metal object with a thin coating of another metal. Electroplating is used to cover metal objects with a coating of a more expensive metal such as silver. The metal object to be plated is made the cathode and a bar of the plating metal, e.g. silver, is made the anode. When electricity is supplied, the silver molecules at the anode lose electrons to form silver ions Ag^+. The silver ions are attracted to the cathode, which is the metal object to be plated. The silver ions gain electrons at the cathode. They change back to silver metal and form a thin layer of silver over the metal object, which is the cathode. See **electrode**, **electrolysis**.

element
a substance that cannot be broken up into simpler substances by chemical reaction. The atoms of an element all have the same number of protons and electrons. There are 92 naturally occurring elements. See **isotopes**.

elementary particles
the different kinds of particles that make up all the matter in the universe.

El Niño
[el **neen**-yo]
originally the name given to a warm ocean current that sometimes appears off the west coast of South America. Today El Niño is used to describe one part of a weather cycle called the El Niño Southern Oscillation, which affects the weather in the Pacific and the whole world. El Niño years bring droughts to some parts of the world and storms and high rainfall to others. An El Niño can last for two or three years. Scientists are not able to predict when an El Niño will begin or end.

embryo [em-bri-oh]
1 a young animal that is growing inside an egg or inside its mother. See **Fig. 33** (p. 110).
2 the part of a seed that grows into the shoot and roots of a seedling.

EMF
see **electromotive force**.

enamel [ee-nam-ul]
the hard, outer layer of a tooth that protects the softer dentine below.

endangered animal
animal whose numbers have been drastically reduced

and is in danger of becoming extinct. Extinction is almost always caused by man's effect on the animal's environment.

endemic
1 a species of plant or animal that is found only in a limited area such as an island.
2 a disease or pest that is always present in an area, such as malaria in tropical coastlines.

endocrine gland
[**end**-o-kryn]
a ductless gland that produces and releases hormones directly into the blood stream of an animal. Examples in humans include the thyroid and pituitary glands and the testes, ovaries and the pancreas. See **hormone**.

endothermic reaction
a chemical reaction that takes in energy during the changing of reactants to products. Endothermic reactions cause a drop in the temperature. The products have more stored chemical energy than the reactants.

energy
the ability to do work. There are two main groups of energy: potential energy or stored energy, and kinetic energy or energy of movement. See **kinetic energy**, **potential energy**.

environment
the physical, biological and chemical conditions in which an organism lives.

enzyme [en-zym]
a complex protein molecule produced in plant and animal cells. Enzymes are catalysts for the many chemical reactions that take place in organisms. See **catalyst**.

epicentre
the point on the Earth's surface directly above the centre of an earthquake.

epidermis
the outer protective cell layer of an animal or plant. See **Fig. 39** (p. 130).

equilibrium
[ee-**quil**-ib-ree-um]
a balanced state. An object that is not moving is in equilibrium because all the forces on it are balanced.

erosion
the process in which broken-up rocks and soil are carried away by water, wind or ice. See **deposition**.

erythrocyte [e-rith-ro-syt]
a disc-shaped, red blood cell with no nucleus. It contains haemoglobin and carries oxygen to all cells.

escape velocity
the minimum velocity that an object must reach to free itself of the Earth's gravitational pull.

essential element
any element that an animal must have in its diet in order to remain healthy. Elements such as copper, iron and zinc are needed for the manufacture of enzymes and proteins. Calcium is needed for bones. See **trace elements**.

ethanol [eth-a-nol]
an alcohol C_2H_5OH, formed from the fermentation of sugars by yeast. Ethanol is the legal recreational drug commonly called alcohol. It is a colourless liquid that burns easily, and is used as a solvent and as a fuel.

eutrophication [you-tr-fi-kay-shn]
a type of pollution in lakes and ponds in which decaying organic matter takes all the oxygen out of the water. This kills fish and other animals.

evaporation
the process whereby a liquid turns into a gas or vapour below its boiling point.

evening star
see **Venus**.

evolution [ee-vo-loo-shn]
a process by which organisms and species change over time. The best explanation to date is based on the theory advanced by Charles Darwin in 1859. It suggests that changes to genes (mutations) that make up the chromosomes cause changes in characteristics that are inherited by the next generation. If these changes improve characteristics, then the new organism has a better chance to survive and reproduce. Many such changes lead in time to new species. See **Darwinism**.

excretion [eks-kree-shn]
the removal of waste products from a living thing. The main substances are carbon dioxide, water and nitrogen-containing compounds. See **kidney, lung, sweat glands, urinary system**. See **Fig. 14** (p. 53).

excretory system [eks-kree-ter-i]
the organs used by complex animals to carry out excretion. See **kidney, lung, sweat glands, urinary system**.

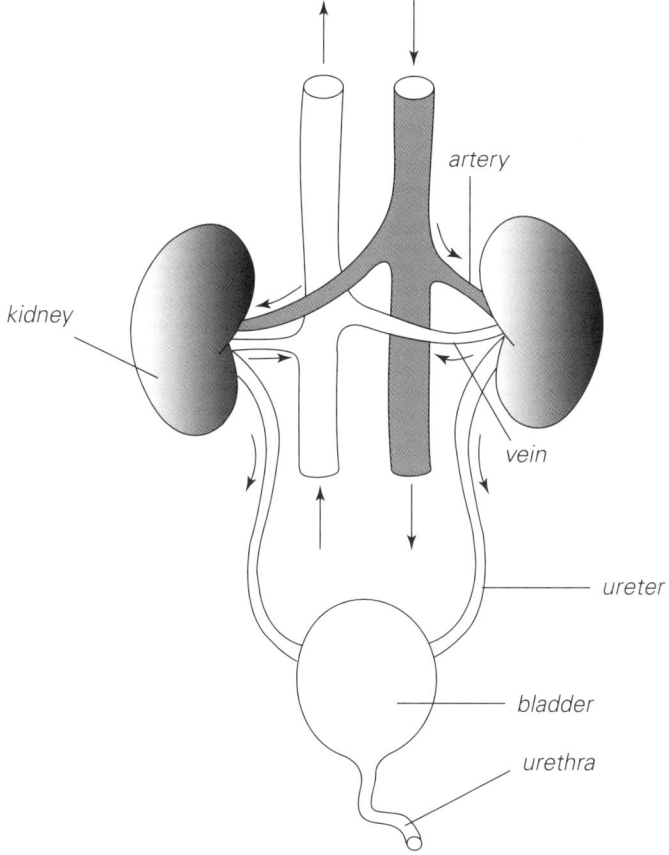

Fig. 14 *the human urinary system*

exocrine gland
a gland, such as the pancreas, which produces chemicals and delivers them to a certain part of an organism through a tube or special opening.

exoskeleton
the hard-jointed case that covers the outside of some animals' bodies. See **arthropod**.

exothermic reaction
a chemical reaction that gives out energy during the changing of reactants to products. Exothermic reactions cause a rise in the temperature. The products have less stored chemical energy than the reactants. Compare **endothermic reaction**.

expand
to get larger. For example, metals expand when they are heated.

experiment
an investigation to discover new information or to test a theory or hypothesis.

exponential growth [**eks**-po-nen-shal]
population growth that depends on the number of individuals present. Growth is slow if numbers are low but increases very rapidly with high numbers.

extension [ex-ten-shn]
the increase in length of, e.g. a spring, when it is stretched by a force.

extinction
the total loss of a species of living things.

extraction [ex-trak-shn]
separating useful materials. For example, pure metals are extracted from ores where they are combined with other elements. See **ore**.

eye
an organ that is sensitive to light and produces images of the environment. See **Fig. 15**.

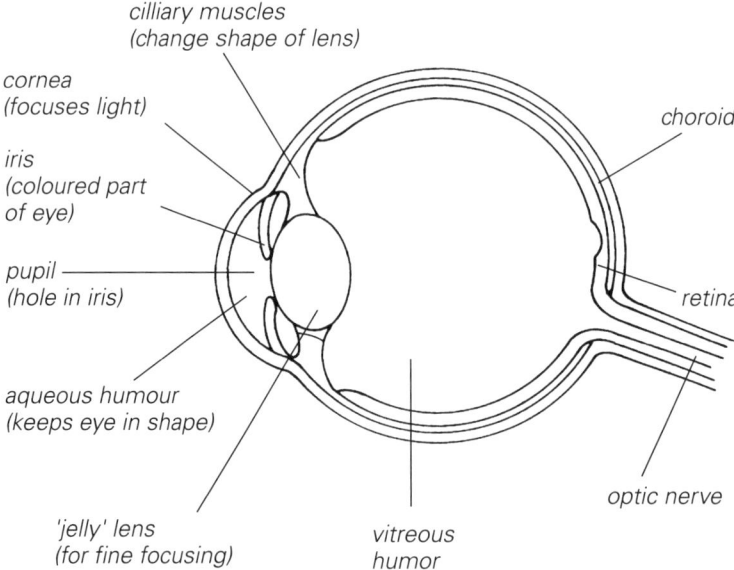

Fig. 15 the human eye

faeces [fee-seez]
the remaining undigested food, and body secretions such as bile and bacteria, that are expelled from the anus.

falling star
the popular name for a meteor that can be seen burning up as it enters the Earth's atmosphere. Also known as a shooting star. See **meteor**.

Fallopian tube
[fa-**loh**-pi-an]
the tube in mammals that carries the egg cells from the ovary to the uterus. Fertilization takes place when sperms from the male meet the egg cell in the Fallopian tube. See **Fig. 38** (p. 129).

fat
a substance made by plants and animals as an energy store. Fats can be changed to carbohydrates and vice versa.

fault
a break in rock layers caused by movements in the Earth's crust.

fermentation
a type of anaerobic respiration carried out by yeast and some bacteria. Ethanol C_2H_5OH is one of the by-products.

fern
type of green plant that reproduces by means of spores. See **frond**.

fertilization
the process in which a sperm and an egg join together during sexual reproduction. Fertilization takes place outside the body in animals that reproduce in water, e.g. fish and frogs. In other animals, the male injects sperm into the female and fertilization takes place inside the body. In plants, the male pollen enters the female ovary and fertilizes the ovules. See **gamete**, **pollination**.

fertilizer
  a substance that is added to the soil to help plant growth. The most important elements in fertilizers are nitrogen, phosphorus and potassium. Compost is a natural fertilizer.

fibre
  1 long cells in plants that provide support. Plant fibre is made of cellulose, which cannot be digested by humans but is an important part of the diet.
  2 any long structures in animals such as muscle and nerve fibres.
  3 synthetic fibres, such as nylon, in which the molecules are long-chain polymers.

fibrous root
  a root system in which a bunch of roots grow from the base of the plant. See **root system**.

field
  the space around an object where a force is exerted. There are different kinds of force fields. There is a gravitational field around any mass. A magnet is surrounded by a magnetic field. An electric field surrounds a charge. In a field, the force increases as you get closer to the object.

fight-or-flight
  the reaction of animals to dangerous situations. The body releases adrenaline to prepare the body either to defend (fight) or run away (flight). See **adrenaline**.

filament
  1 a thin piece of wire with high electrical resistance, such as that in a light bulb. When electric current passes through the wire it heats up, giving off thermal energy and light.
  2 part of the male reproductive organ of a flower. See **stamen**, **flower** and **Fig. 16** (p. 57).

filter
  1 a device for separating solids from liquids and gases.
  2 a semi-transparent sheet that allows light only of certain colours to pass through it. For example, when white light falls on a red filter, blue and green light is blocked but red light passes through.

filter feeder
  an animal that obtains food by filtering small organisms (usually plankton) from the water.

filtration
  a process by which solid particles are removed from a liquid. Filter paper, containing small holes that let the liquid through, but not the solid, is often used.

fish

an aquatic animal that usually has scales all over its body, has gills, and pressure-sensitive lateral lines.

fission

1 binary fission is a type of asexual reproduction in which a single-celled organism divides into two to form two identical individuals.
2 nuclear fission occurs when a heavy nucleus splits to form two smaller nuclei with the release of a large amount of energy. See **nuclear fission**.

flame test

a simple test used to identify the presence of some metals in compounds. A platinum wire is dipped in concentrated hydrochloric acid, then in the compound and placed in the flame of a Bunsen burner, e.g. a lilac flame shows the presence of potassium and a yellow flame shows the presence of sodium.

flight

a form of movement in air. Birds, bats and insects are adapted for flight by having wings and powerful muscles to move their wings. Other animals use skin attached to limbs that open and act like a parachute and let them glide through the air.

flower

a specialised reproductive stem of angiosperms. In most flowering plants, the male and female sex organs are found in the one flower. See **angiosperm** and **Fig. 16**.

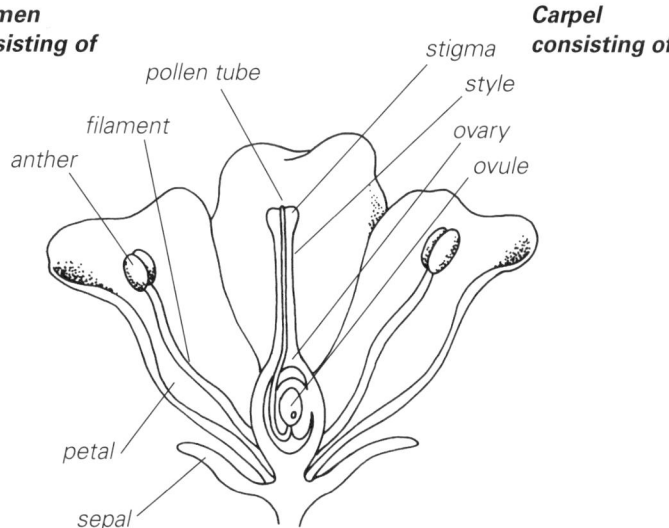

Fig. 16 a typical flower

flowering plant
see **angiosperm**.

fluid
a gas, liquid or finely powdered solid that can flow from one place to another.

fluorine [floo-er-een]
symbol F. A pale, yellow gas element in Group 7 of the periodic table (Z= 9). It is highly reactive and very poisonous.

focal length
the distance from the centre of a lens to its principal focus. See **convex**, **concave**, **principal focus**. See **Figs. 8** and **9** (pp. 32, 36).

focal point
another name for principal focus. See **principal focus**.

foetus [fee-tus]
in mammals, the baby grows inside the mother. In humans, this growing baby is called a foetus after about 8 weeks. Before that time it is called an embryo.

fold
bend in layers of sedimentary rocks, caused by movements in the Earth's crust. Layers bent into a basin shape are called a syncline. Layers bent into an arch shape are called an anticline. See **Fig. 17**.

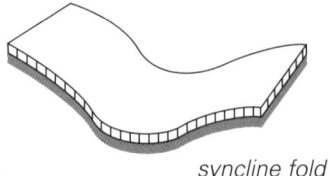
syncline fold

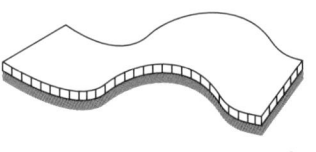
anticline fold

Fig. 17 folding

food chain
a series of organisms in which each organism is eaten by the next in the chain. See **herbivore**, **primary consumer**, **secondary consumer**. See **Fig. 18** (p. 59).

food poisoning
an illness caused by natural poisons or by the presence of disease-causing micro-organisms in food.

food preservation
preventing food from spoiling by adding chemicals or using other methods. Removing water (dehydration or drying) preserves food, as does freezing. Other traditional methods include smoking, packing in salt and pickling. See **artificial preservative**, **acetic acid**.

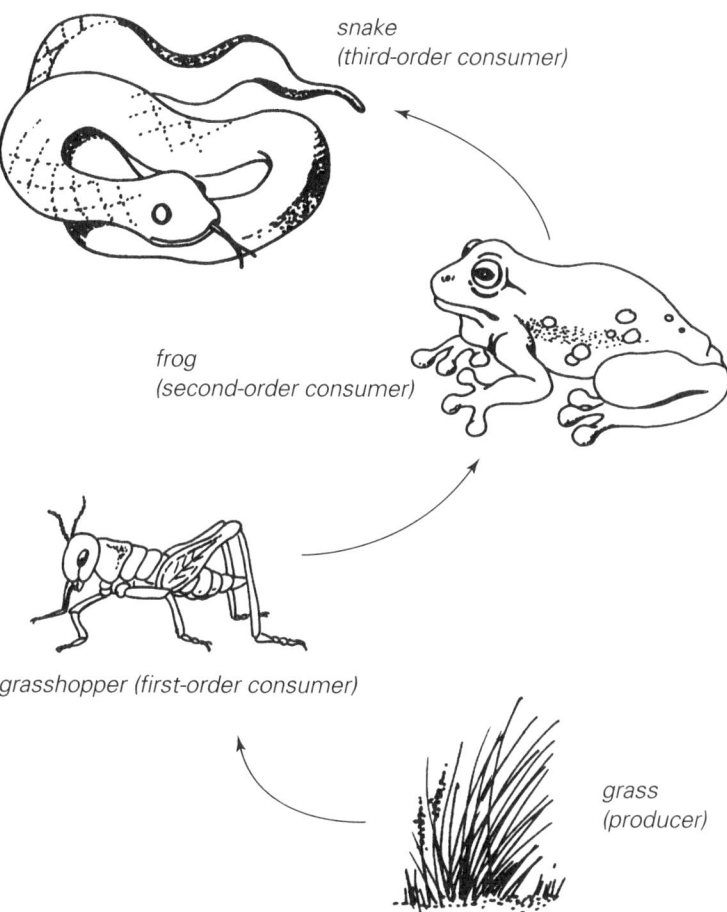

Fig.18 *a food chain*

food web
all the linked food chains in a natural community.

force
a push or a pull that causes an object to speed up, slow down, change direction or change shape.

forensic science
[fer-**en**-sik]
the use of science and technology to gather evidence and solve crime.

forest
a habitat in which trees are the main plants. The Earth's

formula

tropical forests contain many important plant and animal species that are endangered by logging.

formula [form-yoo-la]
an abbreviation using chemical symbols, that shows which elements are in a compound. The formula of an ionic compound such as magnesium chloride $MgCl_2$ shows that there are two chloride ions Cl^- for every one magnesium ion Mg^{2+}. The formula of a covalent compound such as carbon dioxide CO_2 shows that each molecule of carbon dioxide is made up of one carbon atom joined to two oxygen atoms. See **chemical formula**.

fossil
the preserved remains of an organism from the past. Usually only hard parts, such as shells and bones, form fossils. Sometimes, whole animals are preserved, such as insects caught in amber, or animals that are frozen in polar regions.

fossil fuel
fuel such as coal, oil or natural gas, formed from the carbon remains of once-living plants and animals.

fossil record
all the evidence about the past 'recorded' in the fossils trapped in rock layers. The fossil record provides important information about evolution. See **Darwinism, evolution, extinction**.

fovea [fo-vee-uh]
the most sensitive part of the human eye. It is opposite the lens and contains the largest number of cone cells.

fractional distillation
distillation process used to separate a mixture of liquids. Each liquid has its own boiling point. The vapour of the liquid with the lowest boiling point escapes first from the top of the fractionating column and is condensed to form a pure liquid. Other liquids are distilled off as each of their boiling points is reached. See **oil refinery**.

fractionating column
a tall vertical column with trays or beads used in fractional distillation. See **oil refinery**.

freeze
to change a liquid to a solid by cooling.

freeze drying
a method of drying or removing water from a substance at a very low temperature. This method is used to dry substances, such

as enzymes, that would be destroyed if heated.

freezing point
the temperature at which a liquid begins to change into a solid. See **melting point**.

frequency [free-kwen-see]
for a wave or vibration, the number of cycles or waves completed in second. See **wavelength**.

friction
the force that works against two surfaces moving over each other. Friction causes kinetic energy and mechanical energy to be converted to heat energy. Bearings, oil and grease are used to overcome friction between moving parts and improve efficiency of machines.

fronds
the large leaves of a fern. Spores grow on the underside of the fronds.

fruit
the ripened ovary of a flower. Fruits form when the ovules of a flower are fertilized by pollen. The fertilized ovules become seeds.

fuel
1 a substance that burns and can be used as a source of heat (thermal) energy.
2 a nuclear fuel is a radioactive substance such as uranium or plutonium that decays inside a nuclear reactor, producing heat (thermal) energy.

fulcrum [ful-krm]
the point around which a lever turns.

full Moon
see **phases of the Moon**.

fungus
a type of simple land plant that does not contain chlorophyll (pl. fungi). They include moulds, mushrooms, toadstools. Some are decomposers, others are parasites. Fungi produce spores for reproduction.

fuse
a safety device to stop large electric currents in circuits. A fuse is a thin wire in the circuit that heats up and melts, breaking the circuit and stopping the flow of electricity. See **circuit breaker**.

fusion
1 another word for melting.
2 nuclear fusion occurs when two light nuclei join together to produce a heavier nucleus with the release of a great deal of energy. See **nuclear fusion**.

galaxy [gal-ak-si]
a collection of millions of stars and dust, in the shape of a disc with spiral arms. There are many millions of galaxies in the Universe. The next nearest galaxy to our own is two million light years away. See **Milky Way**, **Universe**.

gall bladder [gawl]
an organ under the liver that stores bile. See **bile**, **duodenum**.

galvanized iron
sheets of iron (steel) coated with zinc to prevent rusting.

galvanometer [gal-van-**om**-it-er]
an instrument for measuring small amounts of electric current.

gamete [gam-eet]
the sex cell of an organism that reproduces sexually. The nucleus of gametes contains one half of all the pairs of chromosomes. The sperm cell and ova are gametes formed by animals. The pollen cell and the ovules are gametes formed by plants.

gamma radiation
high energy, electromagnetic radiation given out from some radioactive nuclei. Gamma radiation can pass through more than 25 mm of lead.

gas
a state of matter in which the molecules spread out and completely fill their container. Moving fast (high kinetic energy), the particles collide with each other and the walls of the container, causing pressure.

gas exchange
the passage of a gas across a membrane while, at the same time, another gas passes in the opposite direction. In the lungs,

oxygen and carbon dioxide are exchanged. See **alveolus, lung**.

Geiger counter [gy-ger]
an instrument for measuring nuclear radiation.

gene [jeen]
a portion of a chromosome inside the cell of an organism. Pairs of genes control the characteristics of an individual. Offspring inherit their characteristics from the genes they inherit from their parents. See **chromosome, DNA**.

generation
the members of a family that are about the same age. Parents form one generation and their children the next.

generator
a device that converts mechanical energy into electrical energy.

genetic engineering
[je-net-ik]
changing the genes in organisms so that they produce useful substances or organisms with improved characteristics. For example, bacteria have now been made to produce hormones, vaccines and vitamins. Crops have been changed to make them resistant to disease and farm animals changed to make them grow faster. See **Appendix 5**.

genetics [je-net-iks]
the study of heredity and variation in living things.

geological time scale
[jee-o-**loj**-i-cal]
a time scale that covers the Earth's history.

geology [jee-ol-o-ji]
the study of the origin, structure and composition of the Earth.

geomagnetism
to do with the Earth's magnetic field.

geostationary satellite
[jee-o-**stay**-shn-eri]
a satellite placed in an orbit 35 800 km above the Earth so that it completes one orbit in 24 hours. Because the satellite and the Earth rotate at the same rate, the satellite is in a fixed position relative to the Earth's surface. See **communication satellite**.

geothermal energy
[jee-o-**therm**-al]
heat (thermal) energy that comes from the hot and molten rocks beneath the Earth's surface.

germanium
[jer-**may**-ni-um]
symbol Ge. A hard metallic element (Z=32) used in the electronics industry to make semi-conductors.

germination
[jer-**min**-ay-shn]
the first stages of growth in a seed.

gestation [jes-**tay**-shn]
the period of time in animals between fertilization of an ovum and birth of the offspring. In humans, gestation is called pregnancy and lasts about 40 weeks.

gill
the respiratory organ used by animals that obtain oxygen from the water they live in. Fish have gills.

glacier [**glay**-see-a]
a huge mass of very slow moving ice.

gland
a group of cells that produce a special chemical substance. See **endocrine gland, exocrine gland**.

glass
a transparent solid made by heating a mixture of lime (calcium oxide), soda (sodium carbonate) and sand (silicon oxide).

global warming
a rise in the average temperature of the Earth and its atmosphere believed to be caused, at least in part, by the increase of greenhouse gases resulting from burning fossil fuels in factories and power stations. Global warming may melt polar ice, causing sea levels to rise and flooding of low-lying land.
See **greenhouse effect**.

glucose [**gloo**-kohz]
a white crystalline solid $C_6H_{12}O_6$ found in all plants and animals. It is also called dextrose. It is a high-energy carbohydrate sugar made by plants during photosynthesis. Glucose is used by plants and animals as a source of energy during respiration. See **starch, glycogen, cellulose**.

glycogen [**gly**-ko-jen]
a carbohydrate polymer, made by animals to store energy in the liver and muscles. It is made by joining clusters of glucose molecules. See **insulin**.

gold
symbol Au. A soft, yellow metallic element (Z = 79). It is chemically unreactive and does not corrode in air.

gonorrhoea [gon-o-**ree**-a]
a common sexually transmitted disease, curable with antibiotics.

gram
symbol g. A unit of mass equal to 1/1000th of a kilogram.

granite
a hard crystalline igneous rock. See **igneous rock**.

granulocyte
[gran-yool-oh-syt]
any white blood cell that contains granules. See **leucocyte**.

graphite
an allotrope of carbon. It is one of the few non-metals that conducts electricity. It is a soft, black, slippery solid, often used as electrodes.

gravitational acceleration
the acceleration of a body falling towards the Earth, caused by the force exerted on the body's mass by the Earth's gravity.

gravitational collapse
the collapse of a star under the effect of its own force of gravity. Black holes are formed when very large stars collapse.

gravitational field
the space around a body where any mass will be affected by a force of attraction. The larger the mass of the body, the stronger the gravitational field. The force decreases as one moves away from the centre of the body.

gravity
the tendency of all masses to attract all other masses. Used commonly to refer to the force between the Earth and all things near it.

greenhouse effect
the trapping of thermal energy (heat) radiated by the Earth that would normally escape back into space. Human activity has increased the amount of carbon dioxide in the air and this has trapped more energy inside the atmosphere. See **global warming**.

greenhouse gas
any gas in the atmosphere that absorbs thermal energy radiated from the Earth. Carbon dioxide and methane are the most important greenhouse gases. See **global warming**.

groundwater
water that has soaked underground and become trapped beneath the Earth's surface in permeable rocks.

group
see **periodic table**.

growth
an increase in the weight and volume of an organism by cell division.

guard cell
see **stoma**.

Haber process
[**har**-ber **pro**-ses]
an important industrial process in which nitrogen is combined with hydrogen to make ammonia, NH_3.

habitat
the place where an organism lives, e.g. a pond, the seashore, the canopy of the rainforest.

haemoglobin
[heem-o-**gloh**-bin]
a chemical found in red blood cells in vertebrates, and in the plasma of some invertebrates. The molecule contains iron atoms and is related chemically to chlorophyll. It carries oxygen. When not carrying oxygen it is pale red. When oxygenated it is bright red and called oxyhaemoglobin.

haemophilia
[heem-o-**fil**-i-a]
an inherited disease in humans, causing the blood to clot slowly. The gene for the disease is carried on the Y chromosome. See **sex chromosomes**.

hair
threads of dead cells produced on the skins of mammals.

hair follicle
the tube-shaped depression in mammals' skin that contains the root for hair production. Hair follicles come from tissue underneath the skin.

half-life
the time taken for half the nuclei in a sample of a radioactive material to undergo a nuclear change. The half-life for any particular isotope is constant. See **decay**, **carbon dating**.

Halley's comet
a comet that is visible from the Earth every 76 years. The last visit was in 1986.

halogen [hal-o-jen]
an element of Group 7 of the periodic table. See **fluorine**, **chlorine**, **bromine**.

hard water
water that contains dissolved calcium Ca^{2+} and magnesium Mg^{2+} ions. Hard water forms a scum with soap and produces very little froth or bubbles. The main cause of hardness is the presence of calcium hydrogencarbonate $Ca(HCO_3)_2$ that is formed in limestone regions.

heart
a hollow muscular organ that pumps blood through the circulatory system by regular contractions. See **Fig. 19**.

heat
the thermal energy contained in a body.

heat radiation
see **infra-red radiation**.

heat transfer
heat can move from a hotter part of a solid to a cooler part by conduction. In a fluid, heat is transferred by convection. Heat can also move through empty space by radiation. All hot objects emit infra-red radiation.

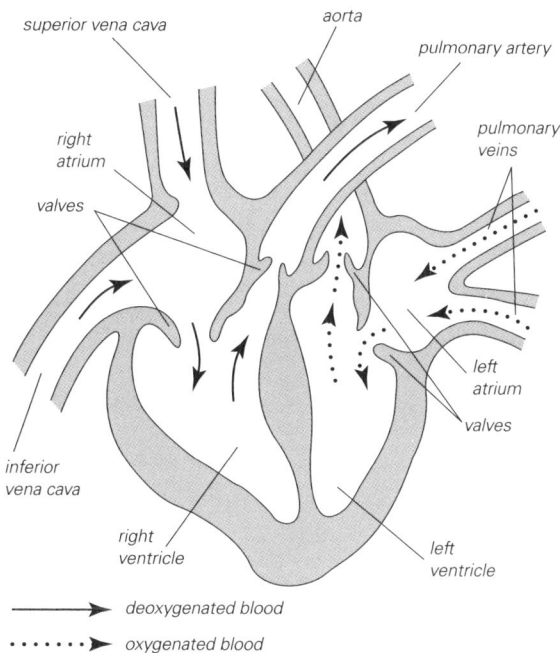

Fig. 19 the human heart

helium [hee-li-um]
symbol He. A colourless, odourless gas element (Z =2). See **noble gases**.

herbivore
an animal that eats plants. See **consumer**.

heredity [he-**red**-i-ti]
the passing on of characteristics, from parents to offspring, through the genes that make up the chromosomes.

hibernation [hy-ber-nay-shn]
a sleep-like state that some animals use to pass the winter months. It is a way of surviving cold temperatures and a lack of food.

HIV
the abbreviation for human immunodeficiency virus; the virus that causes AIDS. See **AIDS**.

HIV positive
having antibodies against the HIV virus (antigen) in the blood. This means that the person has already been infected by the HIV virus. See **AIDS**.

homeostasis [ho-me-o-**stay**-sis]
the tendency of the body to keep internal conditions constant. For example, the human body's internal temperature is kept at about 37°C by mechanisms such as sweating (cooling) and shivering (warming).

hominid [hom-i-nid]
a member of the primate family *Hominidae*, which includes humans and their fossil ancestors.

homoiotherm [hom-**oi**-o-therm]
an animal that can keep its body temperature constant. Mammals (body temperature between 36–38°C) and birds (body temperature between 38–40°C) are homoiotherms. Heat released during respiration is used to replace heat lost through the skin. Compare **poikilotherm**.

hormone [**hor**-mohn]
a chemical produced by the endocrine glands that flows through the blood and controls functions such as growth and reproduction.

host
an organism that provides food and shelter for another organism. See **parasite**.

humidity
a measure of the amount of water vapour in the atmosphere. Warm air can hold more water vapour than cold air.

humus [hew-mus]
organic material in soil formed from dead and rotting plants and animals.

hybrid
an organism produced by the mating of parents with different characteristics.

hydraulic [hy-**drol**-ik]
moving mechanical energy from one place to another using liquids under pressure.

hydrocarbon
a compound that contains only hydrogen and carbon atoms. Methane CH_4, a colourless inflammable gas, is the simplest hydrocarbon.

hydrochloric acid
[hy-dro-**klor**-ik] a strong acid, HCl is made by dissolving hydrogen chloride gas in water.

hydroelectricity
electricity produced by a generator, powered by a water turbine driven by moving water. See **renewable energy**.

hydrogen
symbol H. A colourless, odourless gas element (Z =1). There are three isotopes of hydrogen. See **acid, deuterium, hydrocarbon, water**.

hydrogen chloride
a strong-smelling, fuming gas HCl that dissolves in water to form hydrochloric acid.

hydrogen sulphide
a colourless gas H_2S that smells like rotten eggs. Present in volcanoes, hot springs and other geothermal activities.

hydrosphere [hy-**dros**-feer]
all the water on the Earth's surface including the water vapour in the atmosphere.

hydroxide [hy-**drok**-syd]
compounds containing metal ions and hydroxide (OH^-) ions, e.g. sodium hydroxide NaOH and magnesium hydroxide $Mg(OH)_2$. See **alkali**.

hygrometer [hy-**grom**-it-er]
an instrument used to measure the humidity of the atmosphere.

hypha
a tiny thread that is the building block of all fungi.

hypothermia
[hy-**po**-ther-me-uh] a condition in which the body's internal temperature drops below its normal value of 37°C. Old people are particularly at risk in cold weather. It can cause death.

hypothesis [hy-**poth**-i-sis]
a statement (pl. hypotheses) which we believe to be true but which has not yet been proved by experiment. See **laws, theories and hypotheses**.

igneous rock [ig-ni-us]
rock formed by the cooling of magma. Igneous rocks are crystalline and examples include granite and basalt. See **magma**.

image
the picture formed by a lens or an optical instrument such as a microscope or a camera.

imago [im-**ay**-goh]
the name given to the adult insect that has completed metamorphosis. See **larva**, **pupa**, **metamorphosis**.

immune response
the ability of an organism to produce antibodies.
See **antigens**.

immunity
the ability of an organism to produce antibodies that destroy a disease-causing micro-organism that has entered its body.
See **immunize**.

immunize
to inject a vaccine or serum into an animal to protect it from a disease. A vaccine consists of disease-causing micro-organisms that have been made harmless. When injected, this causes the body to make antibodies to destroy the micro-organisms. The body also remembers how to make the antibodies again if the real disease-causing micro-organism enters. This is called active immunity. Serum is part of the blood from an animal or human that already has immunity to a disease and therefore contains antibodies. This gives the body the ability to protect itself for a short time and is called passive immunity.
See **acquired immunity**.

incisor [in-sy-zer]
a flat chisel-like tooth in the front of the mouth used for cutting food. See **Fig. 43** (p. 144).

incubation
[ink-yoo-**bay**-shn]
the process of keeping the fertilised eggs of birds and some reptiles at the right constant temperature so that the embryo develops successfully.

index fossil
the fossil of an animal that lived only in a particular geological time and can therefore be used to date the age of the rocks in which they are found.
See **ammonite, fossil record**.

indicator
a substance that is one colour in an acid solution and a different colour in a base solution. Also called an acid base. See **litmus**.

inert
a description of a substance that does not easily take part in a chemical reaction.

inert gas
the old name for the elements in Group 0 of the periodic table: helium, neon, argon, krypton, xenon. Now more correctly known as the noble gases. See **noble gases**.

inertia [in-er-sha]
the property of a body that causes it to resist any change in its motion. Thus a body at rest will stay at rest and a body in motion will remain in motion, unless they are acted on by a force.

infra-red radiation
invisible electromagnetic radiation. All hot objects emit infra-red radiation. See **electromagnetic radiation**.

ingestion [in-jest-yn]
the taking of food into the body. For example, putting food in the mouth and swallowing. See **egestion**.

inheritance [in-heri-tns]
characteristics of offspring (children) received from their parents. For example, eye colour is inherited. See **allele, chromosome, gene**.

inorganic compound
generally, any compound not containing carbon atoms, e.g. water H_2O, sodium chloride $NaCl$, magnesium sulphate $MgSO_4$. However, there are some exceptions. For example, the oxides of carbon CO and CO_2 are usually included in inorganic chemistry. See **organic compound**.

insect
a type of arthropod with three body parts: the head, thorax and abdomen. All insects have six legs, and most have wings attached to the thorax. Insects include

flies, butterflies, wasps and beetles.

insoluble
a substance that does not dissolve in a solvent; the opposite to soluble. Salt is soluble in water but insoluble in alcohol.

insulator [ins-yoo-lay-ter]
a substance through which heat (thermal energy) or electricity cannot easily flow.

insulin [ins-yoo-lin]
a hormone made in the pancreas. Insulin causes the liver to remove sugar from the blood and store it as glycogen. See **diabetes**, **glycogen**.

internal combustion engine
an engine that burns fuel and converts the heat (thermal energy) into movement (kinetic energy).

interplanetary space
the space in the solar system between the Sun and the planets.

intestine [in-test-een]
the part of the digestive system between the stomach and the anus. Digested food is absorbed into the blood through the walls of the intestine. See **alimentary canal** and **Fig. 1** (p. 5).

intrusive rock
rock formed by the cooling of magma that has forced its way up from the interior of the Earth, through cracks in the Earth's crust.

invertebrate [in-vert-i-brt]
an animal without a backbone. Invertebrates include arthropods, coelenterates, molluscs and worms.

in vitro [in vi-troh]
describes a biological process that is made to take place outside a living organism, in a laboratory. (*In vitro* means 'in glass'.) For example, *in vitro* fertilization means that an egg is fertilized by a sperm outside of the mother's body.

in vivo [in vi-vo]
describes a biological process that is investigated whilst it takes place inside a living organism.

iodine [I-o-deen]
symbol I. A dark violet, non-metallic element (Z=17). It is an essential element needed by organisms. In humans it is used by the thyroid gland. Iodine is used as a stain and turns a blue-black colour when mixed with starch. See **thyroid**.

ion [I-on]
an atom or group of atoms that has gained a charge by either losing or gaining electrons, e.g. a sodium ion Na^+ has a positive charge and a chloride ion Cl^- has a negative charge.

ionic bond [I-on-ik]
the force of attraction between cations (positively charged ions) and anions (negatively charged ions). See **chemical bond**.

ionic compound
a compound made up of positively and negatively charged ions, e.g. calcium carbonate is made up of positive calcium ions Ca^{2+} and negative carbonate ions $(CO_3)^{2-}$. Ionic compounds have high melting points and conduct electricity when molten or in solution.

ionizing radiation [I-o-nyz-ing]
high-energy particles such as alpha particles and beta particles and high-energy radiation such as gamma rays and X-rays that change chemical compounds by causing ions to be formed. Small amounts of such radiation cause mutations in living things. Large amounts cause illness and death.

ionosphere [I-on-us-feer]
the top layer in the atmosphere from 50 km to over 1000 km above the Earth's surface that contains charged particles (ions).

iris
the coloured ring of muscles in the eye. There is a hole in the centre of the ring, the pupil, through which light enters the eye. The iris can adjust the size of the pupil to let more or less light into the eye. See **Fig. 15** (p. 54).

iron
symbol Fe. A silvery, metallic element (Z=26). It is an essential element needed in small quantities by organisms. An economically important metal. See **steel**, **blast furnace**.

irradiation [i-ray-di-ay-shn]
exposure to any form of radiation. The word is more often used in relation to exposure to ionizing radiation. Irradiation may be used to kill off cancer cells.
See **cancer**, **ionizing radiation**.

isomer [I-so-mer]
two or more chemical compounds that have the same chemical formulae but different structures and therefore different properties. For example, the compound pentane C_5H_{12} can have straight-chain molecules or they can be branched. See **Fig. 20**.

isotope [I-so-tohp]
atoms of the same element that have different mass numbers. For example, a normal carbon atom has 6 protons and 6 neutrons in its nucleus (mass=12). A radioactive carbon atom has 6 protons and 8 neutrons in its nucleus (mass=14). See **carbon dating, deuterium**. See also **Fig. 21**.

```
   H  H  H  H  H              H  H  H  H
   |  |  |  |  |              |  |  |  |
H— C— C— C— C— C— H       H— C— C— C— C— H
   |  |  |  |  |              |  |  |  |
   H  H  H  H  H              H  |  H  H
                               H— C— H
                                  |
                                  H
```

Fig. 20 two isomers of pentane C_5H_{12}

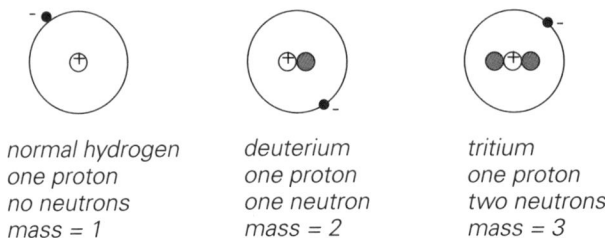

normal hydrogen
one proton
no neutrons
mass = 1

deuterium
one proton
one neutron
mass = 2

tritium
one proton
two neutrons
mass = 3

Fig. 21 the three isotopes of hydrogen

jet propulsion
movement caused by the action of force produced by discharging a jet of gas or liquid. The movement is in the opposite direction to the jet of fluid. See **Fig. 22**.

joint
the point of contact between bones. Some joints like those in the skull bones allow no movement. Others like the elbow allow hinged movement, while shoulder and thigh joints are very flexible. See **ball and socket joint**, **cartilage**, **ligament**.

joule [jool]
symbol J. A unit of energy and work. One joule of work is done when a force of one newton moves a distance of one metre.

Jupiter
the fifth and largest planet in the solar system, having an orbit between Mars and Saturn. There are 16 natural satellites (moons) orbiting Jupiter. See **Appendix 4**.

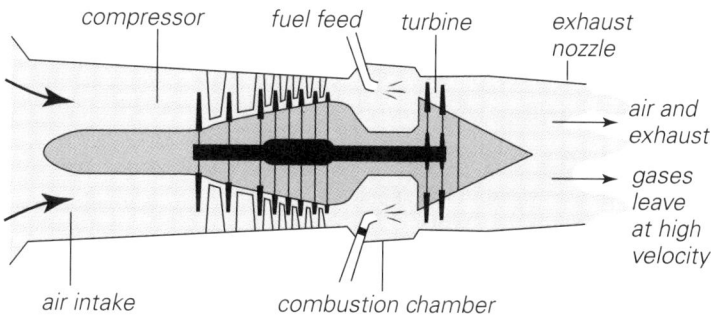

Fig. 22 a jet engine

Kelvin

a temperature scale used by scientists that starts at absolute zero, the lowest temperature possible. One degree Kelvin (K) is equal to one degree Celsius (°C). Absolute zero is equal to –273°C. See **absolute zero**.

kidney

one of a pair of organs in vertebrates, involved in eliminating waste nitrogen compounds such as urine, and in controlling water balance. See **excretion** and **Fig. 14** (p. 53).

kilogram

symbol kg. The standard unit of mass, equal to one thousand grams.

kilowatt [kil-a-wat]

unit of power, symbol kW, equal to 1000 W. See **watt**.

kilowatt hour

symbol kWh. The commercial unit used to measure electrical energy. It is the amount of energy used when an appliance rated at 1000 watts is used for one hour.

kinetic energy

the energy of a moving object. Kinetic energy (k.e.) depends on the mass and the velocity (speed) of the object according to the formula given below. When a moving object comes to a complete stop its kinetic energy is converted to other forms of energy, e.g. heat, light and sound.

$$k.e. = \frac{1}{2} mass \times velocity^2$$

kinetic theory

the theory that explains the behaviour of solids, liquids and gases by considering them to be made up of moving particles. See **Fig. 23**.

kingdom

one of the major groups into which living things are classified, e.g. the animal kingdom and the plant kingdom.

krypton [krip-ton]

symbol Kr. A colourless gas element in Group 0 of the periodic table (Z=36). See **noble gases**.

Heating causes the particles to gain energy and move faster →

← *Cooling causes the particles to lose energy and move slower*

in a solid, the particles are close together and vibrate about a fixed point

in a liquid, the particles are close together and move around slowly

in a gas, the particles are far apart and move around at high speed

melting →
← freezing

evaporating →
← condensing

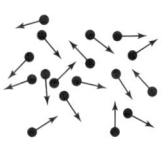

Fig. 23 *kinetic theory of matter*

larva
> a feeding stage in the life cycle of invertebrates. The larva hatches from the egg and does not look like the adult. The larva changes into a pupa. A caterpillar is the larva of a butterfly. See **life cycle**, **metamorphosis**.

larynx [la-rinks]
> the upper part of the trachea (windpipe) of vertebrates. In mammals, reptiles and amphibians, the larynx contains the vocal cords that make sound when air passes through them.

laser [lay-zer]
> a device that produces an intense, highly focused beam of electromagnetic radiation of a specific wavelength.

latent heat
> the amount of heat absorbed or released when substances change state. For example, when 1 g of ice at 0°C melts to give 1 g of water at 0°C, heat is taken in though the temperature does not rise. Similarly, when 1 g of water at 0°C freezes to give 1 g of ice at 0°C, the same amount of heat is given out even though the temperature does not drop.

lateral root
> a smaller root that has branched outwards from the main tap root. See **root system**.

lattice
> the regular structure of particles found in, for example, metals and crystals. See **crystal**.

lava
> molten material that flows from a volcano. Lava cools to form rock. See **magma**.

law of conservation of energy
> see **conservation of energy**.

law of conservation of mass
see **conservation of mass**.

law of conservation of momentum
see **conservation of momentum**.

laws, theories and hypotheses
in science, a law is a rule that is true for all examples; a theory is an idea that explains observations, e.g. the kinetic theory; a hypothesis is a theory or a law that has not yet been proved by experiment.

leaching
washing away of plant nutrients by rain water draining through the soil. Removal of forests can resulted in severe leaching and the loss of soil fertility.

lead [led]
symbol Pb. A dense, dull grey metal element (Z=82).

lead-acid cell
an electrochemical cell made from two lead electrodes in sulphuric acid. The batteries used in cars and trucks are lead-acid cells. Lead-acid cells are secondary cells and can be recharged by passing electricity through them. See **accumulator**, **cell**.

leaf
a flat structure growing from the stem of plants. The cells of leaves contain chlorophyll, which is used in photosynthesis. Holes called stoma are found on the bottom surface and are involved in transpiration. See **photosynthesis**, **transpiration** and **Fig. 24** (p. 80).

lens
a curved piece of transparent material that can form an image of an object. Lenses are usually made of glass or clear plastic. See **concave**, **convex**.

leucocyte [lew-ko-syt]
an amoeba-like colourless cell with a nucleus, found in blood. (Also called white blood cell.) A leucocyte produces antibodies and moves through walls of blood vessels to get to the site of injury or infection.

lichen [ly-ken]
an organism consisting of an alga living inside a fungus. The alga produces food for the fungus by photosynthesis. The fungus protects the alga. See **symbiosis**.

life cycle
the changes that take place in animals or plants, from a fertilized egg to an adult able to reproduce. Humans have a simple life cycle in which the young is similar to its parents. Insects have a more complex life cycle. See **metamorphosis**.

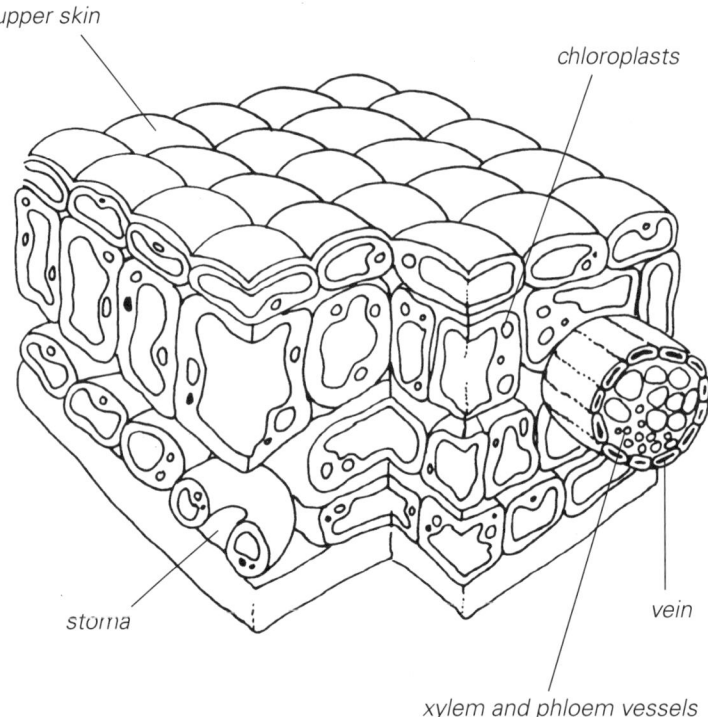

Fig. 24 *section of a leaf*

ligament
> tough tissue that connects one bone to another bone in a joint.

light
> that part of the electromagnetic spectrum to which the eyes of animals are sensitive. White light is a mixture of red, orange, yellow, green, blue, indigo and violet light.

light-dependent resistor (LDR)
> light-sensitive electronic component that has a lower resistance in the light than in the dark. Used for automatic light switches.

light-emitting diode (LED)
> electronic component that lights up when a small current passes through it. Used in electronic displays.

light energy
see **electromagnetic energy**.

light year
a unit for measuring distance in the universe. A light year is the distance travelled by light in one year and is about 9.5 million million km!

lightning
the flash of light associated with thunderstorms caused by the movement of a large amount of electrical energy from the atmosphere to the Earth's surface.

lime
see **calcium oxide**.

limestone
see **calcium carbonate**.

limewater
a colourless solution of $Ca(OH)_2$ in water. See **calcium oxide**.

limewater test
when carbon dioxide gas is bubbled through limewater (calcium hydroxide solution) a milky suspension of insoluble calcium carbonate is formed. This is used to test for the presence of carbon dioxide gas.

$$Ca(OH)_2 + CO_2 \longrightarrow CaCO_3$$
(white precipitate)

If carbon dioxide continues to be bubbled into the limewater, the white suspension disappears as soluble calcium bicarbonate is formed.

lipase [lip-ayz]
an enzyme secreted by the pancreas. It acts as a catalyst in the breakdown of fats.

lipid
the group of substances found in organisms that are not soluble in water and includes all fats and oils.

liquid
the state of matter in which the substance is in the form of a runny fluid. A liquid sinks to the bottom of the container, maintains its volume and has a flat surface. The particles in a liquid are closely packed but are able to move freely past each other.

lithosphere [lith-o-sfeer]
the Earth's solid, rocky crust. Sometimes the word is also used to include the mantle and the core.

litmus
a water-soluble substance that is coloured red in acid conditions and blue in alkaline conditions. See **indicator**.

litre

symbol l. A unit for measuring volume. It is the volume of a cube 10 cm × 10 cm × 10 cm. In chemistry, the unit cubic decimetre dm^3 is often used. $1 dm^3$ is the same as one litre.

liver

a large gland that opens into the alimentary canal. Its functions include the production of bile, the breaking down of proteins to form urea, the storage of carbohydrate as glycogen, the storage of vitamins and minerals, and the breaking down of haemoglobin and toxic chemical compounds. See **Fig. 1** (p. 5).

liverwort [liv-er-wert]

a group of small plants that grow in damp places. They have no roots and stems, do not have flowers and look like flat leaves growing on the ground. Liverworts reproduce by spores.

longitudinal wave

[**long**-dee-tude-in-al] a wave in which the source vibrates in the direction that the wave moves. Sound waves are longitudinal. See **transverse wave**.

long-sightedness

an eye problem that causes the images of near objects to be focused behind the retina, making them seem blurred. Distant objects are focused clearly.

lubrication [loo-bri-cay-shn]

the use of a substance (a lubricant) to prevent contact between solid surfaces moving over each other. This reduces friction, wear and overheating.

luminescence

[loo-min-**ess**-ens] the production of light by substance that is not hot. The light is caused by the release of a photon of electromagnetic energy. Bioluminescence is the production of light by living things such as fireflies.

lunar eclipse

see **eclipse**.

lung

an organ used by land animals for breathing. Mammals have two lungs contained in the thorax. See **alveolus**, **bronchus**, **trachea**, **breathing**. See also **Fig. 25** (p. 83).

lymph [limf]

a liquid, much like blood plasma, that drains from around tissues and is transported by the lymphatic system. The lymph eventually enters the bloodstream near the heart.

lymph nodes

lumps of tissue that are found at various parts of the lymphatic system. Lymph in the lymphatic system flows through the lymph nodes that filter out bacteria and other foreign particles.

Lymph nodes also produce lymphocytes.

lymphatic system
[lim-**fat**-ik]
a network of tubes that carry lymph from cells and tissues back towards the heart.

lymphocyte [lim-fo-syt]
white blood cells (leucocytes) with a large nucleus. Produced in the lymph nodes, they are important to the body's defence against infection.

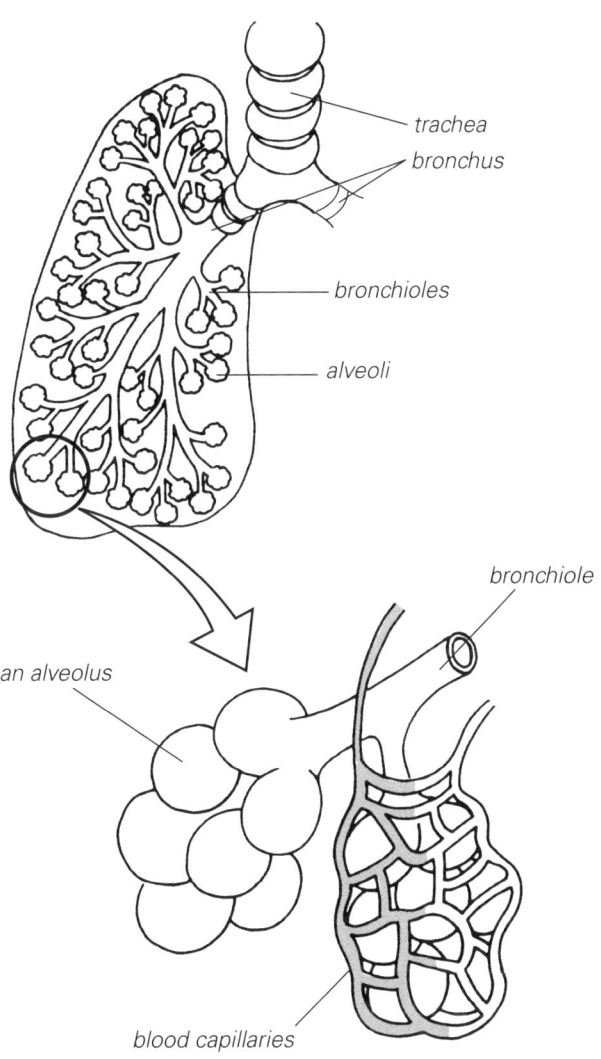

Fig. 25 the human lung

machine
a device that makes mechanical work easier. Machines overcome a large force called the load, by the application of a smaller force called the effort. The six simple machines are the lever, wedge, inclined plane, screw, pulley and wheel.

magma
hot molten rock that comes from deep within the Earth. When magma cools, it forms igneous rocks. Magma that forces its way to the Earth's surface is called lava. Most magma cools to form igneous rocks under the Earth's surface.

magnesium
symbol Mg. A silvery metallic element in Group 2 of the periodic table (Z=12). Magnesium burns in air with a brilliant white light.

magnet
an object that will attract other pieces of iron or steel and repel other magnets. A magnet has two magnetic poles and is surrounded by a magnetic field. See **electromagnet**.

magnetic compass
see **compass**.

magnetic field
the space around a magnet where magnetic forces can be detected.

magnetic pole
the point at which the magnetic field seems to enter or leave a magnet. A magnet has a north pole and a south pole. Like poles of two magnets repel each other. Unlike poles attract each other. The north-seeking pole of a compass needle points towards the north pole of the Earth.

magnetic tape
a plastic tape coated in powdered magnetic material such as iron oxide. The tape

is used to record data in tape recorders and computers.

magnetism
a property of matter that causes magnetic fields.

magnetosphere
[mag-**net**-os-feer]
a comet-shaped magnetic field around the Earth that helps shield the Earth from the charged particles (solar winds) given off by the Sun.

male
an individual who produces male sex cells or gametes. See **gamete**.

malnutrition
[mal-new-tri-shn]
not having enough of the right kind of food. Can be caused by a lack of protein, carbohydrates, fats or vitamins.

mammal
see **Mammalia**.

Mammalia [ma-**may**-li-a]
the mammals. A class of vertebrate animals that are warm blooded, have hair and feed their young on milk. All mammals give birth to live young, except platypuses and spiny anteaters, which lay eggs.

mammary gland
[**mam**-er-i]
a gland in female mammals that produces milk.

mantle
the region of the Earth between the crust and the core. The mantle consists of molten rock moving slowly in convection currents.

marble
a type of rock that contains mainly calcium carbonate and some magnesium carbonate. Pure marble is easily cut and polished and therefore a valuable decorative building material.

Mars
the fourth planet in the solar system, having an orbit between Earth and Jupiter. It has a thin atmosphere of carbon dioxide with a small amount of nitrogen, argon, oxygen and water vapour. Mars has two small natural satellites, Phoebos and Deimos. See **Appendix 4**.

marsupial [mar-**soo**-pi-al]
a sub-class of mammals that includes kangaroos. The female has a pouch into which the young are born at a very immature stage. The young feed from mammary glands inside the pouch. Most modern marsupials are found in Australasia.

mass
the amount of matter in an object. Mass is measured in kilograms. The mass of an object can be measured using a balance or scales. Compare **weight**.

mass number

symbol A. The total number of protons and neutrons in the nucleus of an atom. See **isotope**.

matter

anything that has mass and volume. All objects are made up of matter. Solid, liquid and gas are the three states of matter at normal temperatures. See **plasma**.

measuring cylinder

a transparent container used to measure the volume of samples of liquid.

mechanical advantage

a comparison in machines, of the force moved (load) with the force required to move it (effort).

$$\text{mech. advantage} = \frac{\text{load}}{\text{effort}}$$

mechanical energy

energy produced or used by a machine.

mechanics

the study of the effect of forces on matter.

meiosis [my-oh-sis]

how chromosomes duplicate and then separate to form gametes in the sex organs of plants and animals. Each pair of chromosomes duplicates, then separates to form four gametes each with half the number of chromosomes of a normal cell. See **Fig. 26**.

melt

to change from solid to liquid as a result of heating.

melting point

the temperature at which a pure solid melts. A pure solid will always melt at the

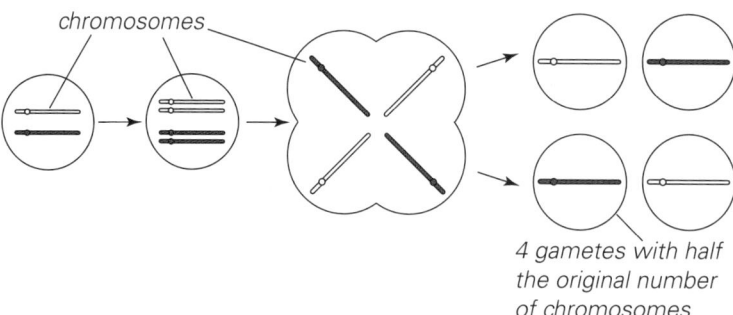

Fig. 26 cell division by meiosis to form gametes

same temperature. Different solids melt at different temperatures. The melting point can be used to identify a pure solid.

membrane
a thin sheet of tissue that covers or supports part of a plant or animal. A cell membrane surrounds all living cells.

meniscus [men-**isk**-us]
the concave or convex curved upper surface of a liquid in a container or tube.

menstrual cycle
[**men**-stroo-al]
a regular monthly change that takes place in the reproductive organs of female humans, apes and monkeys. When the ovary releases an ovum (egg), the lining of the uterus grows thicker with blood vessels preparing for a fertilized ovum. If no ovum is fertilized, then the lining breaks down and flows out through the vagina for 2 to 7 days. During this time a human female is said to be having her period.

mercury
symbol Hg. A heavy, silvery liquid metallic element (Z=80).

Mercury
the first planet in the solar system. Mercury is the smallest planet and has no atmosphere and no natural satellites. See **Appendix 4**.

mesosphere [**mess**-o-sfeer]
the layer in the atmosphere that extends from 50 km to 80 km above the surface of the Earth.

metabolism
[me-**tab**-ol-izm]
all the chemical reactions that take place in a living organism. Digestion, respiration and excretion are examples of metabolic reactions.

metal
a group of chemical elements that are shiny solids and good conductors of heat and electricity. (Mercury is a metal element but is a liquid.) Metal atoms lose electrons to form positively charged ions, e.g. Na^+ and Ca^{2+}. Most metals combine with oxygen to form oxides that are basic.

metamorphic rock
[met-a-**mor**-fik]
one of the three main types of rocks, including igneous and sedimentary rocks. Metamorphic rock is formed

metamorphosis

when existing rocks are changed by heating, increased pressure or by chemical action.

metamorphosis
[met-a-**mor**-fo-sis]
the rapid change from a larva to an adult that takes place during the life cycle of many invertebrates and amphibians. See **Fig. 27**.

meteor [**meet**-i-or]
a streak of light seen in the sky when an object from outer space enters the Earth's atmosphere and begins to burn. Most meteors burn up before reaching the Earth's surface. If a meteor does strike the Earth's surface, it is called a meteorite.

meteorite [**meet**-i-or-ryt]
see **meteor**.

meteorology
[meet-i-or-**ol**-o-ji]
the study of the movement of the gaseous atmosphere and its interaction with the surface of the planet. This information is used to forecast the weather.

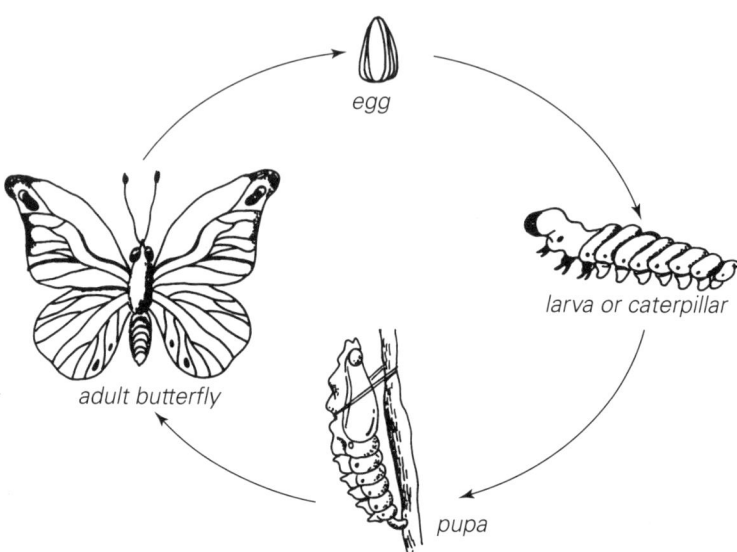

Fig. 27 life cycle of a butterfly

methane [mee-thayn]
symbol CH_4. An inflammable, colourless, odourless gas. The simplest of the hydrocarbons. A molecule consists of one carbon atom forming bonds with four hydrogen atoms. Natural gas, an important fossil fuel, is mainly composed of methane. See **alkane**.

metre
symbol m. A unit of length divided into one hundred centimetres.

metric system
a system of units of measurement started in France in 1791. The system is based on units of 1, 10, 100, 1000 etc. Originally the standard units were the gram for mass, the metre for length and the second for time. Today the standard unit for mass is the kilogram.

microbe
see **micro-organism**.

microbiology
the study of micro-organisms. Microbiology is also an important way to study the chemistry and genetics of all living things.

micro-organism
an organism that can be seen only through a microscope. Bacteria, viruses, protozoans and some fungi and algae are micro-organisms.

microscope
an instrument for forming magnified images of small objects.

microwaves
electromagnetic radiation used to carry communications around the world, using satellites and land-based relay towers. Microwaves are also used in 'microwave ovens' to heat food.

mid-ocean ridge
an underwater ridge of mountains found under the oceans along the fault line of two plates moving away from each other. The ridge is formed by magma rising to the surface and cooling. See **plate tectonics**.

migration [my-gray-shn]
the movement of animals at a particular time or season from one place to another, usually to breed or feed.

Milky Way
the name given to our galaxy. Our Sun is one of more than 100 000 million stars in our galaxy. It is a spiral galaxy and about 100 000 light years in diameter.
See **galaxy**, **light year**.

millibar
a unit for measuring air pressure, commonly used in weather reports. Standard atmospheric pressure is about 1000 millibar. See **Fig. 10** (p. 38).

milligram
symbol mg. A unit of mass equal to one thousandth of a gram.

millilitre
symbol ml. A unit of volume equal to one cubic centimetre. There are 1000 millilitres in a litre.

mineral
a substance found in the ground that can be identified by its chemical and physical properties. Marble, quartz and limestone are examples of minerals. See **ore**, **rock**.

mineral salts
chemicals containing the minerals needed by animals and plants to live and to grow. See **nutrition**.

mirror
a surface that can reflect most of the light that falls on it. A flat mirror is called a plane mirror. See **concave**, **convex**.

mitochondria [my-toh-**kon**-dri-a]
a type of organelle, inside cells, that carries out respiration to produce energy. See **Fig. 7** (p. 25).

mitosis [my-**toh**-sis]
how chromosomes duplicate and then divide, when cells make copies of themselves.

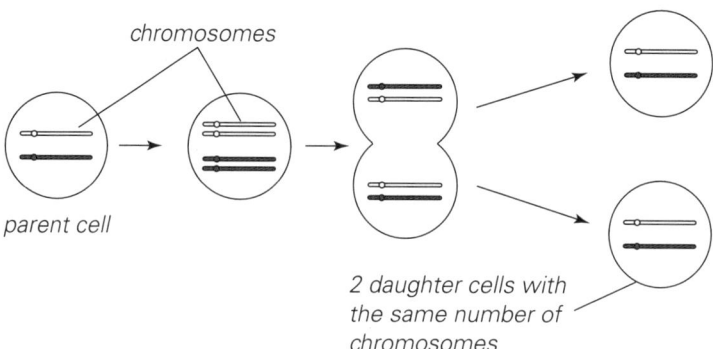

Fig. 28 cell division by mitosis

mixture
two or more different substances mixed together. The substances in a mixture can be separated by methods such as filtration, evaporation and crystallization. A solution is an example of a mixture.

molar
a wide tooth found in the back of the mouth and used for grinding food. See **Fig. 43** (p. 144).

mole
a unit used in chemistry for the amount of matter. 1 mole of any substance contains 6×10^{23} particles. 1 mole of ^{12}C atoms has a mass of 12g.

molecule [mol-i-kewl]
the smallest particle of a compound made up of two or more atoms joined together by chemical bonds.

Mollusca [mol-usk-a]
the molluscs. A group of soft-bodied invertebrates with shells. Snails and oysters are molluscs.

moment
the turning effect of a force about a pivot. The moment depends on the size of the force and its distance from the pivot.

momentum
a property of a moving object, calculated by multiplying the object's mass by its velocity.

momentum = mass × velocity

monocotyledon [mon-o-kot-i-**lee**-don]
one of the two groups of flowering plants whose seeds have one seed leaf (cotyledon). See **dicotyledon, angiosperm**.

monocyte [**mon**-o-syt]
the largest type of white blood cell (leucocyte) that can engulf and destroy bacteria, viruses and cell fragments. See **phagocyte**.

monohybrid cross [mon-o-**hy**-brid]
offspring from parents that both have one dominant and one recessive gene. On average, three out of four of the offspring will show the dominant characteristic. One out of four will show the recessive characteristic.

monotreme [**mon**-o-treem]
a sub-class of mammal that lay large eggs. The duckbill platypus and the echidna are the only living monotremes.

monsoon
tropical wind system that changes direction from south-east to north-west and back again. In tropical regions the monsoon season often brings heavy rains.

Moon
a natural satellite that moves around a planet. Earth has one moon, Mars two and Jupiter sixteen.

moss
a tiny plant that grows in damp places. They have small leaves on the end of stems and have no roots and flowers. They use spores to reproduce.

motion
the movement of an object.

motor
a device that converts other forms of energy into motion.

moulting [mohlt-ing]
1. a seasonal loss of hair and feathers in mammals and birds.
2. the regular loss of the exoskeleton by arthropods, and skin by reptiles, as they grow. See **nymph**.

mucous membrane [mew-kus]
tissue that lines organs of an organism that are open to the outside, e.g. the alimentary canal, lungs and vagina. See **mucus**.

mucus [mew-kus]
a slimy substance that protects and lubricates the mucous membranes in an organism.

muscle
a tissue made up of cells called muscle cells that can contract. Pairs of muscles are attached by tendons to bones across joints. These are called voluntary muscles and can be controlled at will to produce movement. There are also muscles in the walls of blood vessels, heart, alimentary canal, bladder and uterus. These are called involuntary muscles and are controlled automatically by the brain and cannot normally be controlled by will.
See **antagonistic muscles**.

mutation [mew-tay-shn]
a sudden change in a chromosome or gene. Some mutations can cause growth of tumours or cancer. Mutations can occur naturally or be caused by ionizing radiation (X-rays, nuclear radiation) and some chemicals. See **Darwinism**, **evolution**.

mutualism [mew-tew-al-izm]
a relationship between two organisms that need each other in order to survive.

national grid
a network of transformers and cables that allows electricity to be distributed from power stations to all parts of the country.

natural gas
a mixture of hydrocarbon gases formed in the ground usually with petroleum, and used as a fuel. Like petroleum, natural gas was formed by the decomposition of organic matter. See **methane**.

natural selection
see **Darwinism**.

nebula [neb-yoo-la]
a huge cloud of dust or gas in space. Gravity may pull a nebula together to form a star.

nectar [nek-ter]
a sugary liquid produced by some flowers.

nematocyst
[nem-**at**-oh-sist]
a stinging cell found in jellyfish and other coelenterates. When stimulated, it ejects a coiled sting containing a chemical that can paralyse. See **coelenterate**.

nematode [nem-a-tohd]
a type of smooth worm with no body segments. Some nematodes are parasites that cause disease in plants and animals. Microscopic nematodes help break down dead plants and animals.

neon [nee-on]
symbol Ne. A colourless gas element in Group 0 of the periodic table (Z=10). See **noble gases**.

neon lamp
a sealed glass tube filled with neon gas with electrodes at either end. When a voltage is placed across the electrodes, the gas glows with a reddish light.

Neptune
the eighth planet in the solar system, having an orbit between Uranus and Pluto. It has an atmosphere of methane and hydrogen and has two main natural satellites, Triton and Nereid and several smaller moons, which were discovered by the US Voyager probe in 1989. See **Appendix 4**.

nerve
a bundle of nerve fibres. Each nerve fibre is the axon of a nerve cell (neurone). Each nerve cell is insulated by a fatty coating. Nerves connect the nervous system to the organs and tissues of the body.

nerve cell
see **neurone**.

nerve cord
the large bundle of nerves that runs up and down the back of the body inside the spinal column.

nervous system
in animals, the cells and tissues that carry information between all parts of the body. It helps all parts of the body to work together.

neurone [newr-on]
a nerve cell of which the main part is a long thread-like axon that carries an electrical pulse in one direction. Sensory neurones carry information from a sense organ to the central nervous system. Motor neurones carry pulses from the central nervous system to a muscle of a gland. See **Fig. 29** (p. 95).

neutral
1 a neutral solution is not acid or alkali. It has an equal concentration of H^+ and OH^- ions.
2 an object that has no electric charge. A neutral atom has an equal number of negatively charged electrons and positively charged protons.

neutralize
to react an acid with a base (alkali) until the solution is neutral. The products of neutralization are water and a salt. See equation below.

$$H_2SO_4 + CuO \longrightarrow CuSO_4 + H_2O$$
acid   base   salt   water

neutralization
see **neutralize**.

neutrino [new-tree-no]
an elementary particle that has no charge and travels at the speed of light. Neutrinos are thought to have no mass when stationary.

neutron [new-tron]
an atomic particle found in the nucleus of all atoms

except hydrogen. A neutron has a mass of 1 atomic mass unit but no charge.

neutron star [new-tron]
a star that has run out of fuel and collapsed. The pressure is so great that electrons are forced into the nucleus of atoms to join with protons and form neutrons.

new Moon
see **phases of the Moon**.

newton
symbol N. The unit of measuring force. One newton of force gives a mass of one kilogram, an acceleration of one metre per second per second.

Newton's laws of motion
the laws, first set out by Sir Isaac Newton, that describe how bodies move when they are acted on by forces.

Motor neurone

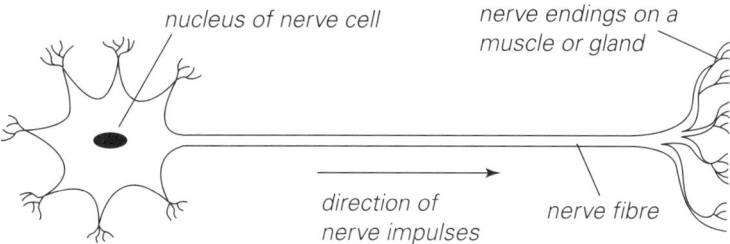

Sensory neurone

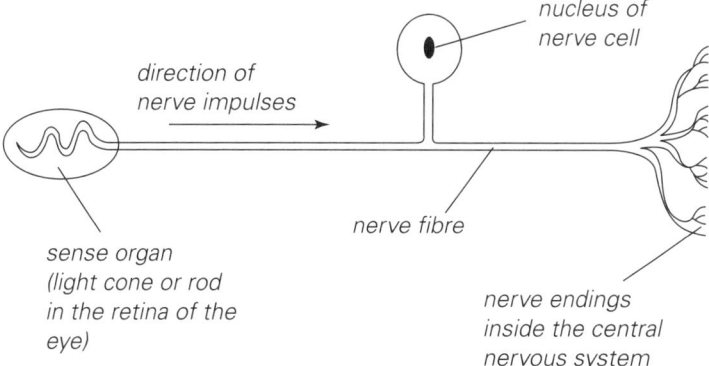

Fig. 29 motor and sensory neurones

nicotine [nik-o-teen]
an addictive drug found in tobacco.

nitrate [ny-trayt]
an ion of nitric acid with the formula NO_3^-. The ion forms salts such as potassium nitrate with positive ions. All nitrate salts are soluble in water and are used by plants for the production of proteins.

nitric acid
a strong acid with the formula HNO_3. It is used in the manufacture of fertilizers, medicines and explosives.

nitrification
[ny-tri-fi-kay-shn]
a chemical process by which nitrogen-containing substances, such as ammonia in animal and plant wastes, combine with oxygen to form nitrates. Nitrates are easily taken in by plants and take part in the production of proteins. This process is carried out by nitrifying bacteria.

nitrifying bacteria
bacteria that convert simple nitrogen compounds into nitrates that can be used by plants.

nitrogen [ny-tro-jen]
symbol N. A colourless odourless diatomic gas element (Z=7). It is the major component of air (about 78%) and is essential for the formation of proteins and nucleic acids in living organisms.

nitrogen cycle [ny-tro-jen]
the movement of nitrogen in nature, between the atmosphere, compounds in the ground and living things. Lightning causes nitrogen and oxygen in the air to combine to form simple nitrogen compounds. Nitrogen-fixing bacteria combine nitrogen and simple nitrogen compounds with oxygen to form nitrates. Plants use nitrates to make proteins. Animals use these proteins. Other bacteria release nitrogen by decomposing dead plants and animals. See **Fig. 30** (p. 97).

nitrogen-fixation
a chemical process in which nitrogen gas in the atmosphere is made to react with other elements to form compounds. Some soil bacteria carry out nitrogen-fixation. Nitrogen-fixation also takes place in the atmosphere during lightning storms. See **nitrogen-fixing bacteria**.

nitrogen-fixing bacteria
bacteria that carry out nitrogen-fixation. Peas, beans and other legumes have bacteria in their roots

that carry out nitrogen-fixation and thus improve soil fertility. See **nitrogen-fixation, nodule**.

noble gases
a group of chemically unreactive gas elements including helium, neon, argon, krypton and radon. They are found in very small quantities in the atmosphere. The noble gases make up Group 0 of the periodic table of elements.

nodule [nod-yool]
the swelling on roots of certain plants that contain nitrogen-fixing bacteria.

non-metal
elements that are not metals and are usually poor conductors of heat and electricity. Non-metal atoms either gain electrons to form negatively charged ions, e.g. Cl^- or share electrons with other atoms to form covalent compounds. Oxides of non-metals are either neutral or basic.

non-renewable energy
see **renewable energy**.

normal
a line drawn at right angles to a surface. See **reflection, refraction**.

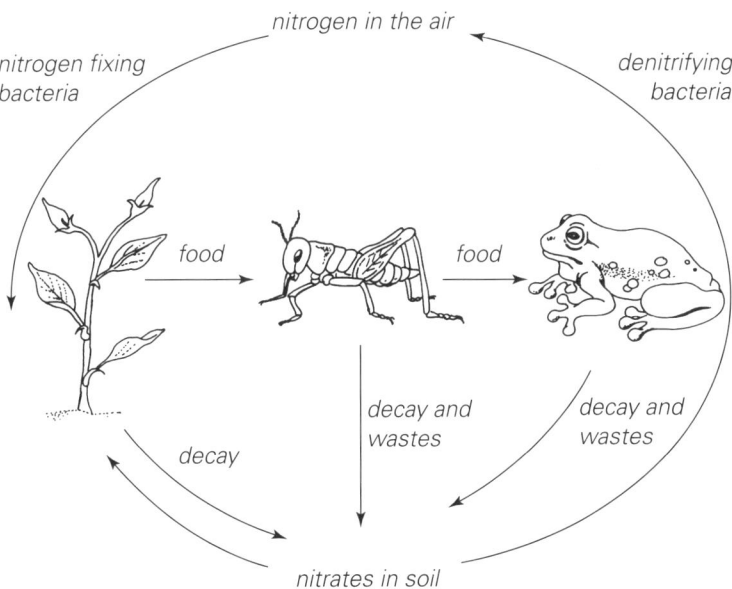

Fig. 30 the nitrogen cycle

nova [noh-va]
a star whose brightness increases over a thousand times, for a few days. Astronomers observe about 15 novas each year. See **supernova**.

nuclear energy [new-kli-a]
energy released during nuclear fission and nuclear fusion. The energy is mainly released as thermal (heat) energy and electromagnetic radiation. Nuclear energy is use to generate electrical energy.

nuclear fission [new-kli-a fish-en]
a nuclear reaction in which the nucleus of a heavy element such as uranium splits into two parts. Two new elements, nuclear radiation and large amounts of energy, are formed.

nuclear fusion [new-kli-a few-zhon]
the joining together of two nuclei to form a larger nucleus. Large amounts of energy are released. The Sun's energy is produced during the fusion of hydrogen atoms to form atoms of helium.

nuclear radiation
alpha, beta and gamma radiation given off when radioactive nuclei decay. It can destroy or damage living cells.

nuclear reaction
a reaction in which a nucleus of an atom changes. See **nuclear fission**, **nuclear fusion**.

nuclear reactor
a device used to produce electricity and/or radioisotopes. Uranium is the usual fuel. Control rods are used to absorb neutrons and thus control the chain reaction. See **chain reaction**, **nuclear energy**, **nuclear fission**.

nuclear waste
see **radioactive waste**.

nuclear weapon
a weapon in which an explosion is caused by nuclear fission, nuclear fusion or a combination of the two. An atomic bomb is the result of nuclear fission. A thermonuclear or hydrogen bomb is the result of nuclear fusion.

nucleic acid [new-klay-ic]
a type of complex organic molecule found in the cells. There are two types of nucleic acids, DNA and RNA.

nucleon [new-klee-on]
a proton or neutron found in the nucleus of an atom. See **proton, neutron**.

nucleon number
the number of atomic particles (protons+neutrons) in the nucleus of an atom. See **atomic mass, isotope**.

nucleus [new-kli-us]
1 the positively charged centre of an atom, which contains most of the mass. The positive charge is carried on protons. All nuclei except the nucleus of the hydrogen atom contain protons and neutrons.
2 the part of most animal and plant cells that contains the chromosomes and is surrounded by a membrane. The nucleus controls the cell. See **Fig. 7** (p. 25).

nutrient [new-tri-ent]
a substance that is taken in and used by a living cell to stay alive. Nitrates, water and carbon dioxide are examples of plant nutrients. Water, carbohydrates, fats, proteins, minerals and vitamins are examples of animal nutrients.

nutrition [new-trish-n]
the process of taking in and using food in organisms. Organisms such as plants manufacture their food from simple substances. Animals and fungi, however, take in complex substances from other organisms. See **metabolism**.

nymph [nimf]
a stage in the life cycle of some insects such as grasshoppers. The nymph looks like the adult. The nymph does not form a pupa but grows into an adult by moulting. See **metamorphosis, moulting**. See **Fig. 31** (p. 100).

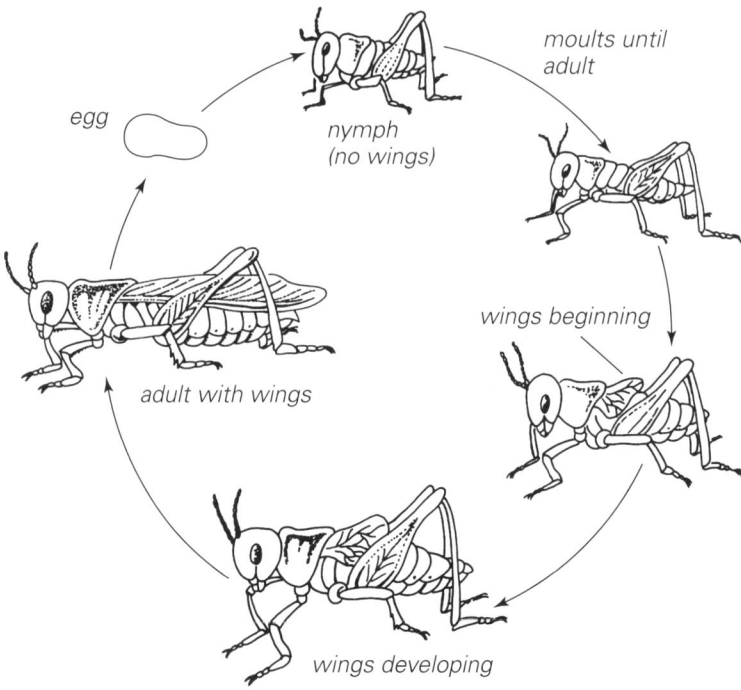

Fig. 31 life cycle of a grasshopper

observation
the skill of noticing the things that happen in an experiment. A record of something that you notice is called an observation.

ocean trench
when an ocean plate meets a continental plate, the ocean plate is forced down under the continental plate. A deep trench is formed beneath the ocean.

oesophagus [ee-sof-a-gus]
the tube that carries food from the mouth to the stomach. See **alimentary canal**.

ohm [*rhymes with* Rome]
symbol Ω. The unit of electrical resistance. If a voltage of 1 volt is placed across a conductor causing an electrical current of 1 amp to flow, then the conductor has a resistance of 1 Ω. See **Ohm's law**.

Ohm's law
a law that states that if the voltage applied across a conductor is doubled, then the electric current flowing in the conductor will also be doubled.

oil
a thick liquid substance that does not dissolve in water. Natural oils in plants and animals are fats that are liquid at room temperatures. Mineral oils found in crude oil consist of hydrocarbons with molecules of between 20 to 30 carbon atoms.

oil refinery
a place where fractional distillation is used to separate useful substances from crude oil. Products include gases (such as methane), petrol, kerosene, diesel oil, lubricant oils, wax and bitumen or tar. See **fractional distillation**.

omnivore [om-niv-or]
an animal that eats both plants and other animals.

opaque [oh-payk]
not letting light pass through. Wood is an opaque material.

optic nerve
the bundle of nerve fibres that takes the nerve messages from the retina to the brain.

optical fibre
a long, thin fibre of glass down which light can pass with little loss of brightness. Optical fibres can be used to carry information such as computer data, telephone conversations and television pictures.

optics
the study of light, its generation, transmission and detection.

oral contraceptive
tablets taken by women to stop pregnancy.

orbit
1 the path taken through space of one object moving around another, e.g. the orbit of the Earth around the Sun.
2 the path taken by an electron travelling around the nucleus of an atom.

ore
rock containing minerals that can be extracted and used in the production of a metal.

ore body
a large amount of ore.

organ
a part of the body of an organism that has its own function. The eye, liver and heart are examples of organs in animals. Leaves and roots are examples of organs in plants.

organelle [or-gan-el]
special structures inside cells including ribosomes, mitochondria and chloroplasts. See **cell**.

organic compound [or-gan-ic]
a carbon compound containing covalent bonds. Carbon atoms have the ability to make four strong covalent bonds and therefore join themselves together in strings and rings. Living organisms are made from organic compounds.
See **inorganic compound**.

organism
any living thing that carries out respiration, excretion and reproduction and responds to an outside stimulus.

orgasm [or-gazm]
the climax of sexual excitement in male and female humans. In males, the ejaculation of sperm takes place during orgasm. Both males and females feel great pleasure during orgasm.

osmosis [oz-moh-sis]
a process that takes place across a selectively-permeable membrane separating two solutions. More solvent passes through the membrane from the weaker solution to the stronger solution. See **selectively-permeable membrane**.

ovary [oh-ver-i]
the organ that produces female gametes. In animals, the ovary produces egg cells. In humans, the ovary also produces hormones. In plants, the ovary produces ovules that grow into seeds after fertilization. See **ovum**, **sexual reproduction**.

oviduct [oh-vi-dukt]
see **Fallopian tube**.

ovipositor [oh-vi-poz-it-er]
an organ at the back end of female insects through which eggs are laid.

ovulation [ov-yoo-lay-shn]
the release of an egg cell from the ovary. In mammals, the egg cell passes down the Fallopian tube into the uterus.

ovule [ov-yool]
the female sex cell of plants that becomes a seed. See **Fig. 16** (p. 57).

ovum
the unfertilized female gamete (sex cell) of a plant or animal that is made in the ovary (pl. ova).

oxidation
the name originally given to a chemical reaction in which oxygen combined with a substance. Now, oxidation is defined as what happens when an atom or group of atoms lose electrons during a chemical reaction. See **reduction**.

oxides
compounds formed between an element and oxygen. See **metal**, **non-metal**.

oxygen
symbol O. A colourless, odourless diatomic gas element ($Z=8$). It is the most abundant element in the Earth's crust. Oxygen in the atmosphere is essential for organisms to carry out aerobic respiration. See **diatomic gas**.

oxygen cycle
the movement of oxygen in nature. In the process of respiration, oxygen from the atmosphere is taken in by living things, combined with carbon and then released back into the atmosphere as carbon dioxide. Carbon dioxide is taken in by plants for photosynthesis. During photosynthesis, oxygen is released back into the atmosphere. In the upper atmosphere, oxygen is converted into ozone by the action of ultraviolet radiation. Ozone also breaks down, back into oxygen. See **photosynthesis**, **aerobic respiration**, **ozone**, **ozone layer**.

oxygen debt
when muscles can't get oxygen quickly enough, the cells start to respire anaerobically. After a while, painful cramps may be felt due to the build up of lactic acid. There is said to be an oxygen debt because more oxygen is needed until the cells can respire normally again. See **aerobic respiration, anaerobic respiration**.

oxygenated blood
[**oks**-ijen-ay-ted]
see **haemoglobin**.

ozone [oh-zohn]
symbol O_3. A colourless gas. It is produced in the upper atmosphere by the action of high-energy ultraviolet radiation on oxygen. See **ozone layer**, **greenhouse effect**.

ozone hole
see **ozone layer**.

ozone layer [oh-zohn]
a layer of the atmosphere between 15 and 50 km above the Earth's surface where oxygen is converted to ozone by high-energy ultraviolet radiation. Most of the ultraviolet radiation from the Sun is absorbed by the ozone layer, thereby protecting living things on the Earth. Skin cancer is one serious disease caused by ultraviolet radiation. In the 1980s it was discovered that holes were appearing in the ozone layer, particularly over the north and south poles. It is thought that these holes are being caused by gases called chlorofluorocarbons. Some refrigerators and aerosols contain chlorofluorocarbons. See **CFC**.

P

palaeontology
[payli-on-**tol**-o-ji]
the study of extinct organisms from their fossil remains.

pallisade cells
[**pal**-i-sayd **sel**-z]
leaf cells containing many chloroplasts where photosynthesis takes place. See **leaf** and **Fig. 24** (p. 80).

pancreas [pank-ri-as]
a gland in vertebrates near the duodenum that produces digestive enzymes, which are secreted into the small intestine. The pancreas is also an endocrine gland producing the hormone insulin. See **Fig. 1** (p. 5).

parallel circuit
[pa-ra-**lel ser**-kit]
an electric circuit in which the electrical pathway branches in such a way that the current has to divide between 'parallel' paths. Compare **series circuit**.

parasite [pa-ra-**syt**]
a living thing that obtains its food from another living thing called the host. Parasites can cause disease. Tapeworms, fleas, lice, skin fungi and the protozoan that causes malaria are examples of human parasites.
See **host**.

parasitism
the process in which one organism (the parasite) lives on or in another organism (the host).

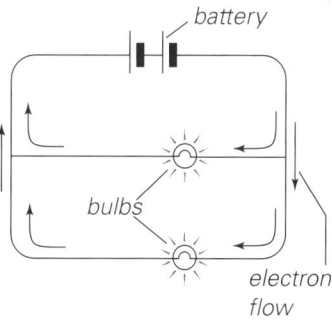

Fig. 32 bulbs connected in parallel in an electric circuit

parent
1 in biology, the male and female partners whose gametes came together to produce an offspring.
2 in geology, the rock from which soil has been formed. The type of soil formed depends on the nature of the parent rock.
3 in physics, a radioactive nucleus that decays to form a different, 'daughter' nucleus.

particle
a small piece of matter. Particles include atoms, molecules, ions and alpha and beta particles. Electrons, protons and neutrons are called fundamental particles.

particle model and theory
a way of explaining the properties of matter in terms of atoms and molecules. See **kinetic theory**.

parts per million (p.p.m.)
a unit used to measure low concentrations such as the concentration of pollutants in air or in water, e.g. a concentration of 1 p.p.m. of a pollutant in air means that there is 1 g of pollutant in every 1000 kg of air.

parturition
[par-tewr-**ish**-on]
the act of giving birth.

passive immunity
immunity acquired by the injection of antibodies from an animal or human that already has immunity to a disease. This occurs naturally between mother and foetus through the placenta or mother's milk. See **acquired immunity**, **immunize**, **immunity**.

passive smoking
the breathing in by non-smokers of tobacco smoke released into the air by nearby smokers.

passive transport
the movement of dissolved substances across a cell membrane by diffusion. It occurs from a region of high concentration to a region of low concentration. It requires no energy.

pasteurization
[**pahs**-cher-ryz-ay-shn]
destroying microbes in milk that could cause disease, by heating the milk to 72°C for 15 minutes and then rapidly cooling it to below 10°C.

patella [p-**tel**-a]
the piece of bone that protects the knee—the 'knee cap'.

pathogen [pa-tho-**jen**]
a microbe that causes disease. Pathogens include viruses, bacteria, fungi and protozoans.

penicillin [pen-i-**sil**-in]
an antibiotic substance made by the mould (fungus) called *Penicillium notatum*. See **antibiotic**, **fungus**.

penis [**pee**-nis]
the male reproductive organ used to pass urine and sperm out of the body. The penis is made up of spongy tissue that can fill with blood and make the penis erect. The erect penis fits into the vagina during intercourse and deposits sperm near the cervix. See **Fig. 38** (p. 129).

penumbra [pen-um-br]
the area of partial shadow caused by an eclipse. See **eclipse**, **umbra**.

peptide
a chain of two or more amino acids joined together. Proteins that are eaten are broken down into peptides during digestion. Peptides are then joined together to form new proteins.

period
1 a horizontal row of elements in the periodic table, each with one more proton in its nucleus. The properties of the elements in a period change gradually from metallic at the left-hand end of the row to non-metallic at the right-hand end of the row.
2 the time taken for a moving object such as a swinging pendulum or an orbiting satellite to return to its original position.
3 see **menstrual cycle**.

periodic table
a table that lists the elements in order of increasing atomic number. The table consists of eight groups of elements and a block of transition metals. The elements in each group have the same number of electrons in their outer electron shell. Group 1 elements are called the alkali metals, Group 7 elements the halides and Group 0 elements the noble or inert gases. See **period**, **alkali metals**, **noble gases**, **electron shell**.
See also **Appendix 1**.

peristalsis [pe-ri-**stal**-sis]
the process of squeezing food along the alimentary canal. Muscles in the wall of the alimentary canal contract and relax to cause the movement.

petrification
[pet-ri-fi-**cay**-shn]
the process in which organic material, such as wood, is slowly replaced by minerals. See **fossil**.

petrochemicals
chemicals produced by processing oil.

petroleum
see **crude oil**.

pH
a scale of numbers from 0 to 14 that shows the strength of an acid or an alkali. Acids have a pH of less than 7. The lower the pH the stronger the acid. Alkalis have a pH of more than 7. The higher the pH the stronger the alkali. A solution with a pH of 7 is neutral. See **indicator**, **neutral**.

phagocyte [fago-syt]
a type of white blood cell that can engulf and destroy bacteria, viruses and other foreign particles that enter the body.

phases of the Moon
the changing shape of the sun-lit surface of the Moon as seen from the Earth. The shape changes as the Moon revolves around the Earth.

phloem [floh-em]
part of the vascular system in plants, consisting of hollow tubes formed by cells joining together in long chains. It carries dissolved glucose and other substances from the leaves, where they are made during photosynthesis, to all parts of the plant. See **Fig. 24** (p. 80).

phosphorescence
[foss-fer-**ess**-ens]
see **luminescence**.

photocell
a device that gives off an electric current (electrons) when light or other electromagnetic energy falls on it. See **photoelectric effect**.

photochemical reaction
a chemical reaction that takes place when light or other electromagnetic radiation provides energy to molecules, causing them to form new substances.

photochemical smog
a form of air pollution in which haze forms over cities. It is caused, in part, by the action of sunlight on gases from car exhausts.

photoelectric cell
see **photocell**.

photoelectric effect
the release of electrons by some substances when exposed to electromagnetic radiation.

photon [foh-tonn]
electromagnetic radiation can be thought of as either a wave of energy or as a stream of energy particles. The energy particles are called photons and have zero mass. Photons are

needed to explain the photoelectric effect. The energy of a photon depends on the frequency of the electromagnetic radiation. See **electromagnetic radiation**, **photoelectric effect**.

photosphere
[foh-toh-**sfeer**]
the visible surface of the Sun or any other star.

photosynthesis
[foh-toh-**sin**-thi-sis]
the process in which green plants make sugars and starches from carbon dioxide and water, in the presence of sunlight. Photosynthesis takes place in the chloroplasts of leaves. Chlorophyll in the chloroplasts trap photons of light energy and convert them into chemical energy.

phototropism
[foto-**tro**-pizm]
the tendency of plants to grow towards the light. See **tropism**.

phylum [fy-lum]
a group of animals with the same characteristics. Humans are in the phylum called vertebrates, which includes all animals with backbones.

physical change
a change in a substance during which no new chemical substances are formed. Changes of state such as melting or boiling are examples of physical changes. Physical changes are usually much easier to reverse than chemical changes.

physics [fiz-iks]
the study of all physical phenomena concerning matter and energy, and the laws that govern them.

pigment
a coloured substance that is insoluble in water. Haemoglobin and chlorophyll are pigments. Melanin is a brown pigment found in skin that gives protection from ultraviolet radiation from the Sun.

Pisces [py-sees]
the fish. There are two groups of fish. One group has skeletons made of bone and the other of cartilage.

pistil
the female sex organ of a flower. See **flower** and **Fig. 16** (p. 57).

pitch
how sounds of different frequencies sound to the ear. Sounds with high

pituitary [pit-yoo-it-eri]
an endocrine gland found underneath the brain. It makes many hormones including the one that controls growth.

pivot
the point about which an object can turn, e.g. a hinge.

placenta [pla-**sent**-a]
the organ in mammals that attaches the growing embryo to the mother. It is made up of blood vessels from the mother and the embryo. The blood vessels are not joined but are very close to each other. The blood of the mother does not mix with the blood of the embryo but dissolved food and oxygen passes from the mother's blood into the blood of the embryo. Waste materials pass from the embryo to the mother's blood. See **Fig. 33**.

planet
a large body in orbit around a star. The Earth, Mars, Venus etc. are planets of our Sun. See **solar system**.

plankton
microscopic animals and plants that are found in fresh or salt water.

plant
living organisms that, with the exception of fungi, make their own food by photosynthesis. Plant cells have cell walls and many contain chloroplasts.

frequencies such as a whistle have a high pitch. Sounds with low frequencies have a low pitch.

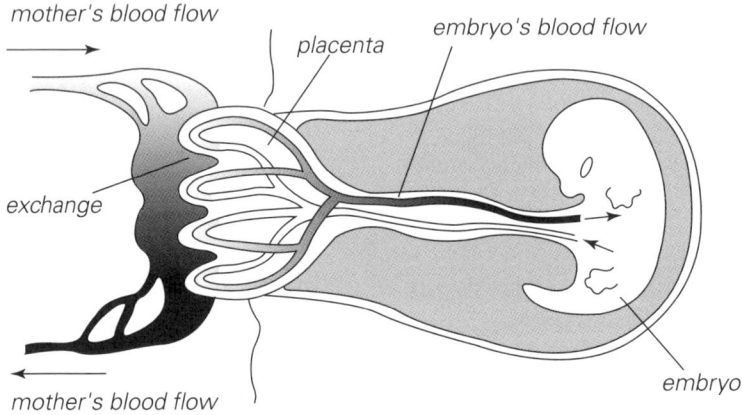

Fig. 33 the human placenta

plasma [plaz-ma]
1. the liquid part of blood when the blood cells are removed. It is a solution of substances such as glucose, amino acids, salts, urea, hormones and substances to help blood clot.
2. a state of matter found at very high temperatures. It consists of free electrons and positively charged ions. Plasma is formed during nuclear fission reactions and at the surface of the Sun.

Plasmodium [plaz-moh-di-um]
a group of protozoa that live in human liver and blood and cause malaria. The anopheles mosquito carries it from one human to another.

plastic
1. a synthetic polymer made from petroleum that can be moulded into various shapes.
2. the description used for a substance whose shape can be permanently changed by squeezing.

plate tectonics
the theory that the Earth's crust is made up of separate solid pieces called 'plates', which have always moved and continue to do so. The theory states that volcanoes, earthquakes and the formation of mountains are the result of plates colliding, rubbing against, or separating from each other.

platelet
a small particle in blood that helps with clotting.

Pluto
the outermost planet in the solar system. It was first observed in 1930. It has one natural satellite called Charon, which was discovered in 1978. See **Appendix 4**.

plutonium [ploo-**toh**-ni-um]
symbol Pu. A dense, radioactive, highly poisonous metallic element (Z=94). Used as a fuel in some types of reactor and also in nuclear weapons.

pneumatic [new-**mat**-ik]
1. an object that contains air under pressure, such as a tyre or ball.
2. a machine, such as a pneumatic drill, that moves mechanical energy from one place to another using compressed air.

pneumonia [new-**moh**-ni-a]
a disease of the lungs caused by bacteria.

poikilotherm
[poi-kil-o-therm]
most animals, except mammals and birds, whose internal body temperature is the same as that of their external environment. Poikilotherms are also called cold-blooded animals. Compare **homoiotherm**.

pole
see **magnetic pole**.

pollen
dust-like male gametes made by flowering plants. See **anther, pollination**.

pollination
the movement of pollen from the male anther to the female stigma in a flower. This leads to fertilization and the formation of seeds. See **Fig. 16** (p. 57).

pollution
the release of substances into the environment that are harmful to humans, other animals and plants. The main pollutants of the air are waste from factories and the exhaust of vehicles. Human faeces, herbicides, insecticides, farm fertilizers and heavy metals are the main pollutants of water.

polymer [pol-im-er]
a substance composed of giant molecules formed by linking many smaller molecules together. See **cellulose, glycogen, plastic**.

polymerization
[pol-im-er-ryz-**ay**-shn]
a chemical reaction in which small molecules link up to form a large polymer molecule.

population
the number of animals or plants of the same species that live in a given area.

potassium
symbol K. A soft, silvery metallic element in Group 1 of the periodic table (Z=19).

potential difference
[po-**ten**-shal]
see **voltage**.

potential energy
[po-**ten**-shal]
the energy stored in an object because of its position. Water at the top of a waterfall, an object held above the ground, a stretched spring and compressed gas all have potential energy.

power
the rate at which work is done or at which energy is converted.

$$\text{power} = \frac{\text{work done}}{\text{time taken}}$$

power station
a place where electrical energy is generated by burning fossil fuels, by converting the kinetic energy of moving water, or from nuclear energy. See **nuclear reactor**.

precipitate [pre-**sip**-i-tayt]
an insoluble substance formed during a chemical reaction between two solutions, e.g. mixing a solution of barium chloride and sodium carbonate produces a white precipitate of barium carbonate. See equation below.

$$BaCl_2 (aq) + Na_2CO_3(aq)$$
$$\downarrow$$
$$2NaCl(aq) + BaCO_3 (s)$$
(insoluble white precipitate)

precipitation
[pre-sip-i-**tay**-shn]
1 all the liquid and solid forms of water formed in the atmosphere. Rain, hail, snow, dew, frost and clouds are forms of precipitation.
2 the formation of a precipitate.

predator
an animal that hunts and eats other animals for food. Predators are secondary and tertiary consumers in the food chain.
See **food chain, consumer**.

pregnancy
see **gestation**.

premolar
a type of tooth used for grinding food. Premolars are smaller than molar teeth.

pressure
the force pressing on one square metre ($1m^2$) of surface area.

$$pressure = \frac{force}{area}$$

primary cell
electrochemical cell that cannot be recharged. Most batteries used to power radios, calculators and torches are primary cells.
See **electrochemical cell**.

primary colour
one of the three colours of light (red, green and blue) that, when mixed together in equal amounts, gives white light. Any colour can be made by mixing different amounts of the primary colours.

primary consumer
see **consumer**.

primary sexual characteristics
physical changes to the reproductive system at puberty. For example, the release of ova (eggs) in girls

Primates

and the production of sperm in boys. See **secondary sexual characteristics**

Primates
a group of mammals that includes monkeys, apes and humans.

principal focus
the point through which parallel rays of light pass, or from which they seem to come, when reflected or refracted by a mirror or lens. See **concave, convex, focal length, focal point**.

proboscis [pro-**boss**-iss]
a long tube-like structure that protrudes from the head of an animal, e.g. the sucking mouth parts of a mosquito or the trunk of an elephant.

producers
green plants. They produce the food and energy for all other organisms in a food chain or web.

product
a substance produced in a chemical reaction.

progesterone [pro-**jest**-er-ohn]
a hormone made by the ovaries in females. It is one of the hormones that controls the menstrual cycle.

program(me)
a set of instructions that enables a computer to carry out a particular task, e.g. a program enables a computer to be a word processor or a games machine.

prostate
a gland found below the urinary bladder in male mammals. It produces some of the substances that make up semen. See **Fig. 38** (p. 129).

protease [proh-ti-ayz]
any enzyme that splits proteins into smaller peptides and amino acids.

protein [proh-teen]
one of a group of substances found in all living organisms. A protein is made up of a chain of amino acids, e.g. the hormone insulin, enzymes and haemoglobin. Plants manufacture their own amino acids and proteins, from nitrates and other ions absorbed from the soil and carbohydrates. Animals make proteins from amino acids produced during the digestion of protein foods. Beans, peas, fish and meat are important body-building protein foods.

proton [proh-tonn]
an atomic particle of mass 1 amu and carrying a positive

charge equal in value to the negative charge of an electron. Protons are found in the nucleus of all atoms. All atoms of an element have the same number of protons, e.g. all atoms of carbon have six protons.

proton number
see **atomic number**.

protoplasm
[**proh**-to-plazm]
the total contents of a living cell. It is made up of the cytoplasm and the nucleus.

protozoa [proh-to-**zoh**-a]
a group of single-cell animals, usually microscopic and mostly saprophytes (organisms that feed on dead organisms).

puberty [**pew**-ber-ti]
the changes that take place as a child becomes a sexually mature adult. See **adolescence**.

pulley
a simple machine consisting of a rope passing over a wheel. A load is applied at one end and an effort at the other. Arrangements of more than one pulley reduce the effort required to move the load. See **Fig. 34**.

pulmonary artery
[**pul**-mon-eri]
the blood vessel that carries deoxygenated blood from the heart to the lungs, where it receives oxygen.
See **Fig. 19** (p. 67).

pulmonary vein
[**pul**-mon-er-i]
the blood vessel that carries oxygenated blood from the lungs to the heart.
See **Fig. 19** (p. 67)

pulse
a wave of pressure that passes through the arteries every time the ventricles of the heart contract. It can easily be felt at the wrist of humans. It is used to measure the pulse rate (the number of times the heart beats in a minute).

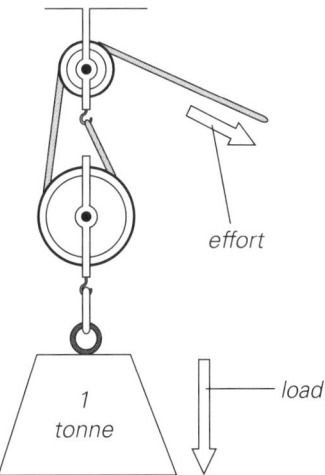

Fig. 34 a double pulley

pumice [pum-iss]
a volcanic rock with many holes and air spaces caused by expanding gases in the lava that formed it. Pumice is sometimes light enough to float on water.

pupa [pew-pa]
a stage in the life cycle of some insects. A larva changes into a pupa. The adult insect emerges from the pupa. A chrysalis is the pupa stage of a butterfly. See **life cycle**, **metamorphosis**.

pupil
the hole at the front of the eye through which light enters. See **iris**.

pyramid of biomass
a diagram showing the total mass of the organisms in each level of a food chain.

pyramid of numbers
a diagram showing the total numbers of the organisms in each level of a food chain. See **Fig. 35**.

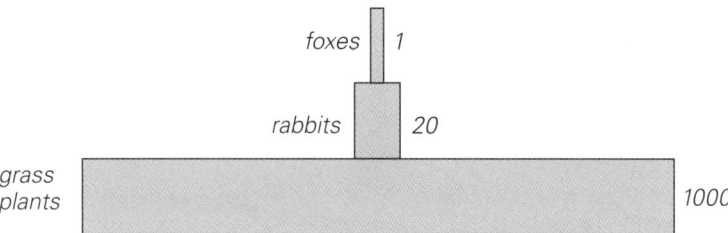

Fig. 35 a pyramid of numbers for the food chain: grass → rabbit → fox

quadrat [kwad-rat]
1 a square piece of ground marked off so that the distribution of plants within it can be studied.
2 a square frame used to select, at random, and mark off areas of vegetation for study.

quantum [kwan-tum]
in physics, a fundamental unit or 'packet' of energy that cannot be divided (pl. quanta).

quantum theory
a theory that explains physical phenomena using the idea that electromagnetic radiation transfers energy in quanta. See **photon**, **photelectric effect**.

quark [kwar-k]
one of six fundamental particles believed to make up particles such as protons and neutrons. Evidence of the existence of quarks comes from making high-energy particles collide in particle accelerators.

quick lime
see **calcium oxide**.

quinine [kwin-een]
a substance extracted from tree bark. One of the earliest substances used in the treatment of malaria.

rabies [ray-beez]
a very serious disease of the central nervous system caused by a virus. Humans may be infected through the bite of an infected animal.

radar
the use of radio waves to locate objects such as an aircraft at a distance. Microwaves are sent out from a rotating transmitter. The waves are reflected off an object such as an aircraft, and return to the transmitter. The time taken for the waves to return, and their direction, give the distance and position of the aircraft.

radiation
1 energy in the form of electromagnetic radiation transmitted through space at the speed of light.
2 a stream of particles such as alpha particles or beta particles that travel at speeds less than the speed of light.

radioactive dating
see **carbon dating**.

radioactive waste
any radioactive solid, liquid, or gaseous material by-products. Nuclear reactors, the manufacture of nuclear weapons and the processing of radioactive ore all produce radioactive waste. Radioactive waste can be very dangerous to living things and can have a half-life of many thousands of years. See **decay**, **half-life**.

radioactivity
the breaking down of the nucleus of some atoms into two smaller nucleii. Alpha particles, beta particles or gamma radiation are also formed.

radio astronomy
the study of radio waves given off by stars and other heavenly bodies.

radio-isotope
[**ray**-di-oh **I**-so-tohp] an isotope of an element that is radioactive. Carbon 14 is a radioisotope of carbon.

radio waves
a range of electromagnetic radiation of different frequencies that are used in radio and television transmission, satellite communication and navigation. See **microwaves**, **radar**.

rainbow
an arc of colour across the sky containing all the colours of the spectrum. A rainbow is seen when sunlight is refracted by rain or the spray of a waterfall.

rainfall
see **precipitation**.

rainforest
an important biological community in which trees are the main plants. The rainfall in a rainforest is usually high. Many of the world's rainforest areas have been, and continue to be, destroyed by logging.

rain shadow
a drier area on the opposite side of a mountain to the rain-bearing winds.

RAM
abbreviation for Random Access Memory, the electronic memory available in a computer for the temporary storage of information. A program such as a word processor or a game uses RAM. When the computer is turned off the information in RAM is lost.

rare gas
see **noble gases**.

rarefaction [rair-i-**fak**-shn]
the reduction in the pressure of a fluid. The opposite of compression.

rate
the amount of change that takes place in a given time.

rate of reaction
the speed at which a chemical reaction releases products or uses up reactants.

reactant
a substance that is changed in a chemical reaction. Reactants are changed into products.

reaction
see **chemical reaction**, **nuclear reaction**, **chain reaction**.

reactivity series
a group of elements or compounds placed in order according to how reactive they are. For example, the metals below are in order of their reactivity with water:

potassium — most reactive
sodium
magnesium
iron
copper
gold — least reactive

reagent [ree-**ay**-jent]
compounds such as sulphuric acid and hydrochloric acid that are used in experiments in a laboratory.

real image
see **image**.

receptor
the end part of a nerve that detects a stimulus such as light, sound, taste, smell, heat, pain or touch.

recessive gene
see **dominant gene**.

recrystallization
a method of purifying a substance. The substance is dissolved in a solvent and then filtered. The solution is allowed to crystallize. The crystals are filtered out and the process is repeated.

recycling
the process by which a used resource is recovered and used again, e.g. when metal is recovered for scrap metal and used again.

red blood cell
see **erythrocyte**.

red giant
a giant star in the last stages of its evolution when most of its fuel has run out. A red giant can be up to 100 times larger than our Sun.

redox reaction
a chemical reaction in which one reactant is reduced whilst another is oxidised. For example:

$$\underset{\text{oxidised}}{\overset{\text{reduced}}{2CuO + C \longrightarrow 2Cu + CO_2}}$$

reduction
the name originally given to a chemical reaction in which oxygen was given off by a substance. Now, reduction is defined as what happens when an atom or a group of atoms gains electrons during a chemical reaction. See **oxidation**.

refining
making a substance purer. Sugar is refined by recrystallization. Crude oil is refined by fractional distillation.

reflected ray

the outgoing ray of light from a mirror or other shiny object.

reflection

the bouncing back from a surface of a wave, i.e. light, sound and other forms of wave energy. The law of reflection states that the incident or striking ray makes the same angle with the normal. The normal is a line at right angles to the surface at the point the ray strikes the surface.
See **Fig. 36**.

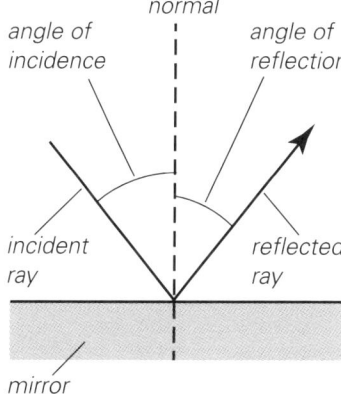

Fig. 36 reflection of light off a mirror

reflex action

the body's very quick, unconscious response to a stimulus. The reaction of the eye's pupil to a flash of bright light is a reflex action. See **reflex arc**.

reflex arc

the pathway of nerves that sends messages to and from the central nervous system so the body can react quickly. See **reflex action**.

refraction

the bending of a light ray as it passes from one medium to another. When light passes from a less dense medium to a more dense medium such as from air to water, the ray is bent towards the normal. Rays passing from a more dense medium to a less dense medium, such as from water into air, are bent away from the normal. See **Fig. 37**.

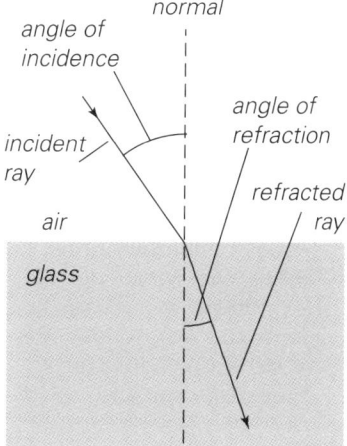

Fig. 37 refraction of light as it passes from air to glass

regeneration
[re-jen-er-**ay**-shn]
the ability of a living thing to regrow injured or lost parts of its body. Plants regenerate leaves, stems and flowers. Some animals such as crabs can replace lost legs. Humans can regenerate liver and blood cells.

relative atomic mass (RAM)
the mass of an element's atoms compared with the standard ^{12}C atom (RAM=12). The table below lists some values:

element	RAM
hydrogen	1
carbon	12
oxygen	16
sodium	23
iron	56
gold	197

relative humidity
the amount of water vapour in the air, compared with the maximum amount of water vapour the air can hold at that temperature. It is expressed as a percentage. Air with a relative humidity of 100% cannot hold any more water vapour.

relay
a magnetic switch, used in electrical circuits, controlled by a permanent magnet or an electromagnet.

renal [ree-nal]
relating to the kidneys, e.g. the renal artery supplies blood to the kidney.

renewable energy
energy resources that can be replaced naturally. Geothermal energy, hydroelectricity, wind power and solar energy are examples of renewable energy resources. Non-renewable energy resources include fossil fuels such as coal, oil and nuclear fuels.

reproduction
the process by which living things produce offspring. See **sexual reproduction**, **asexual reproduction**.

reptile
a cold-blooded land animal with scales. They lay eggs that need incubating. Vertebrate of the class Reptilia.

Reptilia [rep-til-i-a]
the reptiles.

repulsion [re-pul-shn]
a force pushing two objects apart. See **attraction**.

resistance
1 in physics, the property of a substance to impede (work against) the flow of electricity through it. The

resistance of a component is given by:

$$\text{resistance} = \frac{\text{voltage applied}}{\text{current}}$$

2 in biology, the ability of a disease-causing micro-organism to remain unaffected by antibiotics and other drugs.

respiration
the process by which living things break down glucose into simpler substances and release useful energy. Respiration occurs in the cells of animals and plants. See **aerobic respiration**, **anaerobic respiration**.

respiratory organ
[ress-**pir**-a-ter-i]
an organ in animals, such as the trachea in insects, the gills in fish and the lungs in humans, used to take in oxygen and give off carbon dioxide. See **gas exchange**.

retina [ret-in-a]
the inner lining of the eyeball, on which light passing through the lens forms an image. The retina contains cells sensitive to light that are connected to the brain through the optic nerve. See **Fig. 15** (p. 54).

reversible reaction
a chemical reaction that can take place in both directions. For example, ammonia breaks down into hydrogen and nitrogen but nitrogen and hydrogen can join together to make ammonia.

$$2NH_3 \rightleftarrows N_2 + 3H_2$$

Richter scale [rik-ter]
a scale used to measure the energy of earthquakes. The scale is exponential, so an earthquake that measures 7 on the Richter scale is 10 times more powerful than one that measures 6.

Ring of Fire
a zone of volcanoes and seismic activity, 32 500 km long, that encircles the Pacific Ocean.

RNA
controls protein manufacture. It is a nucleic acid (ribonucleic acid), found in the nucleus and cytoplasm of cells. RNA is made by DNA at the chromosomes, and then moves to the cytoplasm.

rock
a solid made from minerals and found on the surface of the Earth. There are three types of rock: sedimentary, igneous and metamorphic.

rock cycle
the change of one type of rock into another, which takes millions of years. Magma produces igneous rocks, which are eroded and then deposited to form sedimentary rocks. These may be changed by heat and pressure to metamorphic rocks. Where sedimentary and metamorphic rocks are forced far underground, they melt and rejoin the magma and so the 'cycle' is complete.

rocket
a device driven by jet propulsion. Rockets are used as fireworks for entertainment, as weapons of war and as space vehicles. See **jet propulsion**.

rod cell
a light sensitive cell in the retina of the eye. Rod cells produce black and white images and are used for seeing in dim light.

ROM
read-only memory. A computer device used to store data that can be read but cannot be changed.

root
the part of the plant that grows downwards into the ground. Roots provide support and are used to store food, e.g. potatoes and carrots. Roots are covered in root hairs that take in water and dissolved minerals from the soil.

root hair
see **root**.

root nodule
see **nodule**.

root system
the arrangement of roots in a plant. There are two types: the tap root system of dicotyledons and the fibrous root system of monocotyledons.

rtp
room temperature and pressure. Used when measuring the volumes of gases. For example, 32g of oxygen takes up 24 litres (24 dm^3) at rtp.

Ruminantia
a group of mammals including cattle, sheep, goats and deer. Ruminants have a four-chambered stomach. In the first chamber (the rumen), micro-organisms secrete an enzyme that helps digest cellulose into useful sugars. See **cellulose**.

rusting
the corrosion of iron or steel to form iron oxides. Water and oxygen are needed for rusting.

safer sex
any sexual activity, such as the use of condoms during sexual intercourse, that reduces the risk of contact with infected body fluids. This gives some protection against sexually transmitted diseases such as AIDS.

saliva [sa-**ly**-va]
a watery substance made by glands around the mouth. It contains an enzyme that begins the digestion of starches.

salt
1 a compound formed when an acid and a base react together.
acid + base ⟶ salt + water
2 name used for sodium chloride (common salt).

saprophyte [sa-pro-fyt]
an organism that feeds on dead organisms. Saprophytes are important in releasing nutrients for plants to use. They are important in the carbon and nitrogen cycles. See **decomposer**.

satellite [**sat**-er-lyt]
an object that moves in orbit around a planet. The Moon is a natural satellite of the Earth. See **artificial satellite**, **geostationary satellite**, **communication satellite**.

saturated
a solution in which no more solute can be dissolved at that temperature.

Saturn
the sixth planet in the solar system, having an orbit between Jupiter and Uranus. It is the second largest planet in the solar system, has about 22 natural satellites and an atmosphere of hydrogen. It is noted for a system of rings surrounding its equator. The rings are believed to be made up of millions of small, ice-covered, rocky particles. See **Appendix 4**.

scalar [skay-lar]
a quantity that has size only but no direction. For example, mass is a scalar quantity. See **vector**.

scales
small bone-like plates that cover the skin of fish and reptiles.

scavenger
an animal that feeds on dead or dying organisms.

scrotum [skroh-tum]
the sac of skin that supports the testes in mammals. The scrotum lies outside the body, keeping the testes at the correct temperature for the production of sperm (i.e. slightly cooler than body temperature). See **Fig. 38** (p. 129).

secondary cell
an electrochemical cell that can be recharged. A car battery is a secondary cell. A secondary cell is recharged by passing electricity through it, in the opposite direction to which it produces electricity. See **electrochemical cell, lead-acid cell**.

secondary colour
a colour formed by mixing together two or more primary colours. Yellow is a secondary colour made by mixing the primary colours red and green.

secondary consumer
see **consumer**.

secondary sexual characteristics
the physical changes that occur at puberty but which are not directly related to the sex organs. For example, the growth of facial hair and the development of a deeper voice in boys. See **primary sexual characteristics**.

sediment
soil particles that are deposited by moving water or wind. Rivers carry a suspension of weathered rock and deposit layers of sediment on the ocean floor. See **deposition, weathering**.

sedimentary rock
[sed-i-**ment**-er-i]
a type of rock formed from particles of other rocks that have been laid down in layers and compressed. Sedimentary rock is usually soft. Sandstone is a sedimentary rock. See **deposition, weathering**.

sedimentation
the process in which small solid particles in a suspension settle to the bottom of the liquid.

seed
the structure of a plant that develops when a female ovum is fertilized by male pollen. The seed contains

some stored food and an embryo that will grow into a new plant. See **cotyledon**.

segmented worm
see **annelid**.

seismic wave [syz-mik]
a wave that carries energy through the Earth away from a sudden underground rock movement. The ground shakes (earthquake) when the wave reaches the surface.

seismograph [syz-mo-grahf]
an instrument used to detect and measure the strength of earthquakes. See **Richter Scale**.

seismology [syz-mol-o-ji]
the study of earthquakes.

selective breeding
See **artificial selection**.

selective logging
the harvesting of some trees from a forest, leaving behind young trees that can continue to grow.

selectively-permeable membrane
a membrane that has microscopic holes that allow only small particles to pass through, e.g. if a solution of glucose is placed in a selectively-permeable membrane, then during osmosis, water molecules would be able to pass through the membrane, but glucose particles would not. Often referred to as a semi-permeable membrane.

semen [see-men]
a liquid made by male animals. It contains sperm. It is released from the penis into the vagina during sexual intercourse and helps carry the sperm to the female ova.

seminal vesicle [**sem**-in-al **vess**-i-kul] a gland in the male mammal reproductive system. It produces the liquid that mixes with sperm to form semen. See **Fig. 38** (p. 129).

semi-permeable membrane
[sem-i-per-mi-a-bul]
See **selectively-permeable membrane**.

sense
what a living organism uses to take in information about its surroundings. Sense organs such as the eyes, ears, skin and nose contain special nerve cells called receptors that are sensitive to light, sound, pressure, pain, temperature and chemicals. See **sense organ**.

sense organ
an organ that contains receptors that are sensitive to external stimuli and send information to the brain. The eyes, nose, ears and tongue are sense organs in humans.

sepal
see **calyx**.

series circuit
an electric circuit in which the parts are connected one after the other. The electric current flows through each part, one after the other. Compare **parallel circuit**.

sewage
organic waste, mainly faeces, dissolved or suspended in water.

sex cell
see **gamete**.

sex chromosomes
the pair of chromosomes associated with the inheritance of sex in animals. There are normally two types, X and Y. The Y is usually smaller. In most animals the female has two X chromosomes and the male has one X and one Y.

sexual intercourse
the insertion of the penis into the vagina followed by ejaculation. Also called coitus and copulation.

sexual reproduction
a way in which new offspring are produced by the joining of a male gamete with a female gamete. This forms a zygote, which can grow into a new organism. See **gamete**, **meiosis**, **fertilization**, **zygote**. See **Fig. 38** (p. 129).

sexually transmitted disease
any disease that is transmitted during sexual intercourse or other sexual contact. The diseases are also called venereal diseases. Having fewer sexual partners, and using condoms, can protect against sexually transmitted diseases. See **AIDS**, **gonorrhoea**, **safer sex**, **syphilis**.

shale
a type of sedimentary rock formed from clay.

shoot
the part of the plant that grows above the ground.

shooting star
see **meteor**.

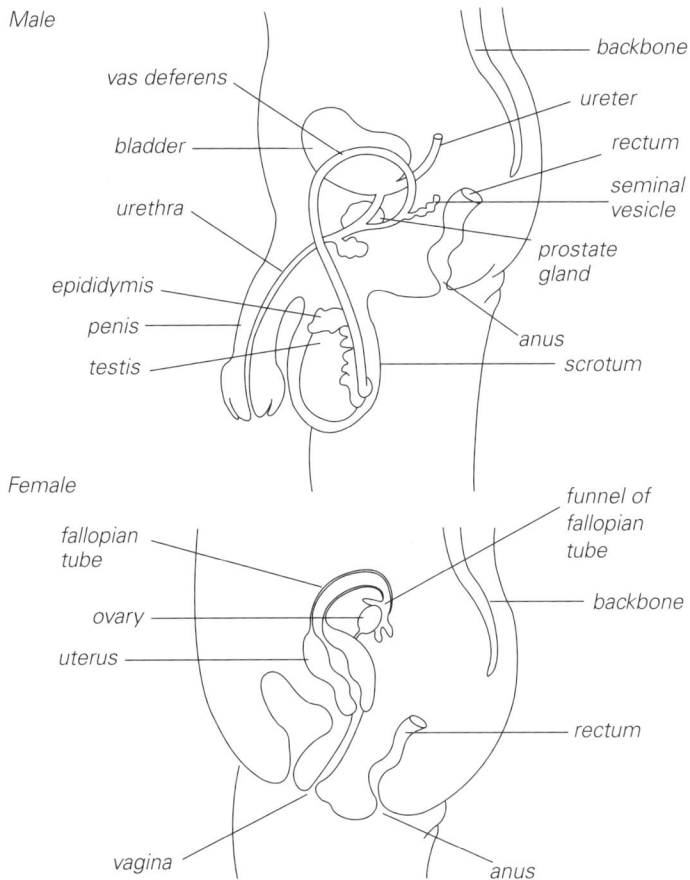

Fig. 38 male and female human reproductive systems

short circuit

a fault in an electric circuit that allows the current to by-pass part of the circuit. This causes a large amount of current to flow, which may damage components and cause a fire.

short-sightedness

an eye problem that causes the images of distant objects to be focused in front of the retina, making them seem blurred. Near objects are focused clearly.

SI units

the standard set of international units for measurement (*Système International*). They include the metre for length, the second for time and the kilogram for mass. See **Appendix 3**.

silicon

symbol Si. A hard element from Group 4 of the periodic table with both metal and non-metal properties. It is the second most common element in the Earth's crust. It is used in the production of semi-conductors for the electronics industry.

silver

symbol Ag. A white, soft metallic element ($Z = 47$).

skeleton

the hard part of animals that supports the body and protects organs. Muscles are attached across joints to allow movement. Some animals have exoskeletons (skeletons outside the body). See **Fig. 40** (p. 131).

skin

the waterproof covering of vertebrates. The outer dermis is made up of dead cells and protects against invading bacteria and the loss of water. The inner dermis is made up of living cells and contains oil glands, hair cells, special receptor nerve cells and blood capillaries. See **sense organs**. See **Fig. 39**.

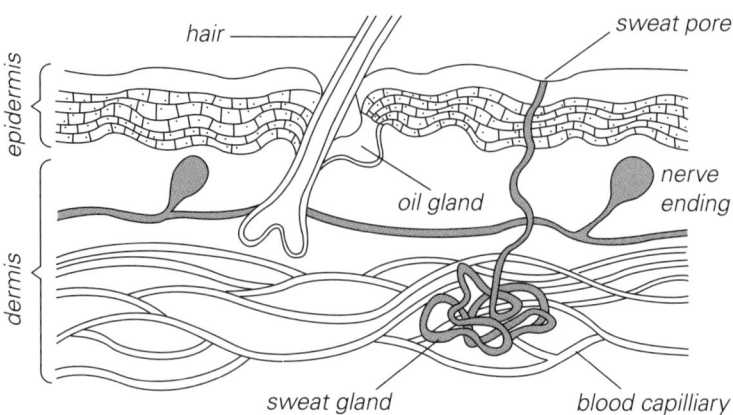

Fig. 39 section of human skin

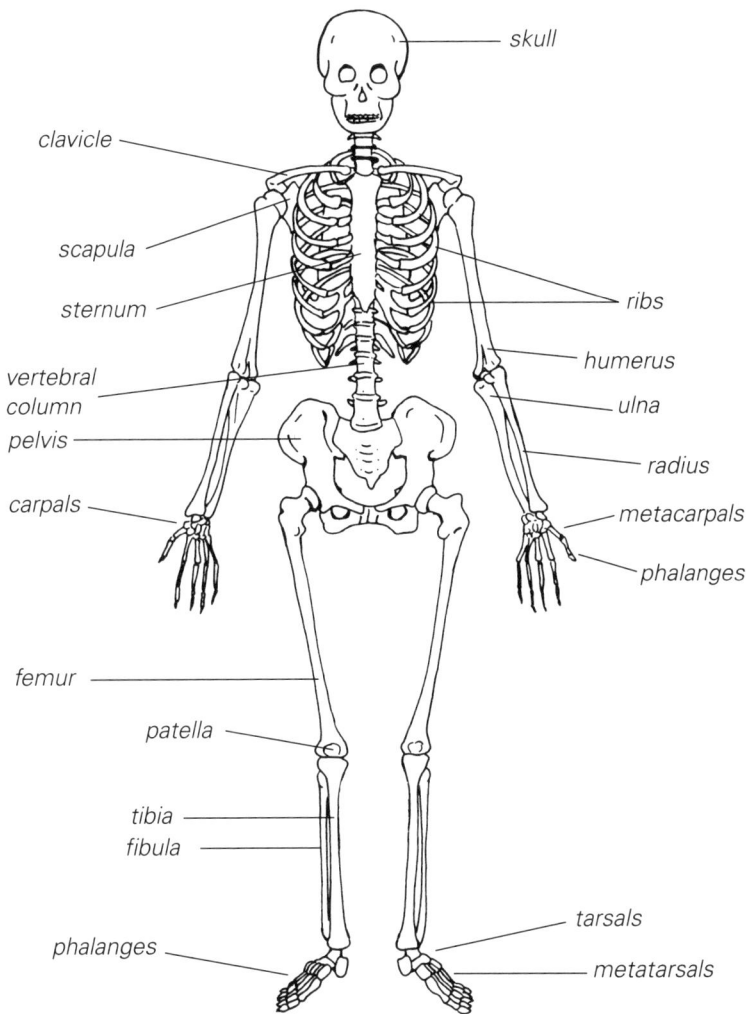

Fig. 40 the human skeleton

slaked lime
see **calcium hydroxide**.

smelting
the process of obtaining a metal from its ore. This usually involves heating the ore to high temperatures.

sodium [soh-di-um]
symbol Na. A soft, silvery, reactive alkali metal element (Z=11), found as a chloride in sea water. It is an essential element for animals, for controlling fluid in cells, and for the nervous

sodium hydroxide

system. Sodium metal reacts violently with water to form sodium hydroxide and hydrogen gas. See **alkali metal**.

sodium hydroxide
[**soh**-di-um **hy**-drok-syd] a white solid NaOH that quickly absorbs water from the air. It is an alkali. As a solid or in solution, it is very corrosive to skin. Commonly called caustic soda. See **sodium**, **alkali**.

soft water
water that contains only very small amounts of dissolved chemicals. Soft water produces a lot of froth and bubbles with soap and does not leave a scum. See **hard water**.

software
the set of instructions (program) used by a computer to perform a task.

soil
a mixture of rock particles, humus, water and air that provides a good environment for plants to grow.

soil erosion
the removal of soil by water or wind. The roots of plants hold the soil together and protect it from erosion. The removal of trees from the forests causes much soil erosion. See **deforestation**.

solar cell
a cell that produces a voltage when sunlight falls on it. The cell contains a material that gives off electrons when sunlight falls on it.

solar eclipse
see **eclipse**.

solar energy
energy from the Sun. All energy on Earth except nuclear energy originates from solar energy. Plants use solar energy for photosynthesis. The water cycle and winds are also powered by solar energy.

solar flare
a sudden eruption of energy on the Sun's surface lasting from minutes to hours. The flare produces radiation and particles. Solar flares disrupt radio signals on Earth.

solar heating
the use of energy from the Sun to heat water for use in, for example, homes. Cold water flows into a collector placed in the sunlight. Energy absorbed heats the water, which then leaves the collector. Hot water is stored for later use.

solar system
> the Sun and everything that moves around it. The solar system includes the planets, their moons as well as all the asteroids and comets. See **Appendix 4**.

solar wind
> a stream of particles that flow into space from the Sun. The particles are mainly protons and electrons. Solar winds cause the tails of comets.

solder [sol-der]
> an alloy of lead and tin that melts at about 250°C. It is used to join metals such as copper tubes, electric wires and components of electronic circuits.

solenoid
> a coil of wire, usually wound around an iron rod, that becomes a magnet when a current flows in the wire. An electromagnet. See **relay**.

solid
> a state of matter that keeps its shape. The particles in solids are close together and remain in a fixed position.

solubility [sol-yoo-**bil**-i-ti]
> the amount of substance that can be dissolved in a fixed volume of liquid at a given temperature.

soluble [sol-yoo-bul]
> describing a substance that will dissolve in a solvent.

solute [sol-yoot]
> the soluble substance that dissolves in a solvent to form a solution. Sugar is a solute that dissolves in the solvent, water, to make a solution.

solution
> a mixture in which a solute is dissolved in a solvent. Sugar is a solute that dissolves in the solvent, water, to make a solution.

solvent
> the liquid in which a solute dissolves to form a solution. Water is a solvent of ionic compounds such as common salt (sodium chloride). Ethanol (alcohol) is a solvent of many organic compounds.

sonar [soh-nar]
> equipment used by ships to find the depth of the water. Sound waves are sent out from a transmitter. The waves echo off the bottom of the ocean and return to the transmitter. The time taken for the echo to return gives the depth of the ocean. This method can also be used by fishing boats to find shoals of fish. Compare with **radar**.

sound
energy that moves as vibrations of different frequencies through matter, and can be detected by the human ear. Younger people can hear a greater range of frequencies than older people. See **pitch, speed of sound**.

space probe
an unmanned space craft that collects information from other planets, moons and bodies such as comets. The information is sent back to Earth as radio signals.

species [spee-sheez]
a group of organisms that are able to breed with each other to produce fertile offspring.

spectrum
a full range of related properties listed in order. A rainbow shows the different colours that make up white light and is called the visible spectrum. See **electromagnetic spectrum**.

speed
a measure of how fast an object is moving or how far an object travels in a given time.

$$\text{speed} = \frac{\text{distance moved}}{\text{time taken}}$$

speed of sound
sound travels at a speed of about 340 metres per second in air at 20°C.

sperm
the gamete made in the testes of male animals. Sperm cells join with ova during fertilization and form a zygote. See **zygote**.

spermatozoa
[sper-mat-o-**zoh**-a]
see **sperm**.

spinal cord
a bundle of nerve cells that runs down from the brain inside the vertebral column. Nerve cells, carrying information to and from the brain, run out from the spinal cord to all parts of the body.

spine
see **vertebral column**.

spiracle [spyr-a-kel]
the small hole in the side of the body of insects and other arthropods. Air enters and leaves the body through the spiracles.

spiral galaxy
see **galaxy**.

spleen
an organ found near the stomach of vertebrates. The spleen is involved in the

blood system. Leucocytes are made in the spleen. The spleen also stores red blood cells and removes old or damaged red blood cells.

spontaneous generation
[spon-**tay**-ni-us]
a belief that somehow living things can be created from non-living matter. This belief has been shown to be wrong.

spore
a type of cell that fungi, mosses and ferns use for reproduction. They are produced by asexual reproduction and do not need to be fertilized.

spring balance
a simple type of balance used to measure force by stretching a spring. The strength of the force is measured by the amount the spring is stretched. A spring balance is often used to measure the weight of an object.

staining
using a dye (stain) to change the colour of colourless biological tissue so that it can be seen clearly under a microscope.

stainless steel
see **steel**.

stalactite and stalagmite
a growth of calcium carbonate found in limestone caves. A stalactite hangs down from the cave roof. A stalagmite grows upwards from the cave floor.

stamen
the male reproductive organs of a flower. Pollen is made in the anther that sits at the end of a thin stalk called the filament. See **flower**.

star
a large celestial body that gives off energy from nuclear fusion. The Sun is a small star giving off energy from the fusion of hydrogen atoms to form helium.

starch
a polymer carbohydrate, made by plants to store energy. Each molecule of starch is made up of chains of glucose molecules joined together. Animals use starch as a source of energy. See **polymer**.

states of matter
solid, liquid and gas are the three physical states in which matter can exist. Plasma is sometimes called a fourth state of matter.

static electricity
an effect caused by charged particles collecting on an object (usually an insulator). Rubbing a plastic rod against a piece of material may give it an electrostatic charge. Lightning is the sudden flow of static electricity between clouds and the ground.

steam engine
an engine that uses high-pressure steam from a boiler to move pistons up and down in cylinders. The moving pistons turn a crank shaft.

steel
an alloy of mainly iron with a small amount of carbon, and sometimes other elements such as manganese, silicon, chromium, molybdenum and nickel. Steel with more that 11% chromium is called stainless steel.

stem
the part of a plant from which the branches, leaves and buds grow.

sterile [ste-ryl]
1 an object that is free from any living micro-organisms is said to be sterile. Doctors make sure all equipment used during an operation is sterile.
2 an organism that cannot reproduce is said to be sterile.

sterilization [ste-ri-lyz-**ay**-shn]
1 the removing of micro-organisms from a wound, food or medical instruments.
2 the operation carried out to make an animal unable to reproduce. See **vasectomy**.

stigma
the sticky part of the female reproductive organ of a flower that receives the pollen. See **carpel, flower**.

stimulus [stim-yool-us]
anything that affects an organism, causing it to respond. Cells called receptors detect the stimulus and send messages along nerves to the brain. Sense organs in animals are receptors for stimuli such as light, sound or touch.

stinging cell
see **nematocyst**.

stoma
a small hole in the underside of leaves (pl. stomata). Carbon dioxide passes into the leaf through stomata. Water vapour and oxygen pass out of the leaf through stomata. See **transpiration**. See **Fig. 24** (p. 80).

stomach
a digestive organ in vertebrates that helps in the digestion of food. The stomach is part of the alimentary canal. It is a muscular bag in which food is mixed with hydrochloric acid and an enzyme called pepsin. These digestive juices are made by glands in the wall of the stomach. See **Fig. 1** (p. 5).

strata
layers or bands of sedimentary rock.

stratosphere [strat-o-sfeer]
the second layer in the atmosphere from about 11 km to 30 km above the surface of the Earth. Most of the dangerous ultraviolet radiation from the Sun is absorbed in the upper layers of the stratosphere.

strong acid
an acid that breaks up completely into hydrogen ions in solution. Sulphuric acid H_2SO_4 is a strong acid. Solutions of strong acids are very corrosive to skin.

structure
a description of the arrangement of the parts of something. The structure of an atom describes the arrangement of subatomic particles in the nucleus and the electrons around it.

style
part of the female reproductive organ of the flower. See **carpel**, **flower**.

subatomic particle
any small particle that comes from within an atom. Protons, electrons, and neutrons are all subatomic.

sublime [sub-lym]
the physical change of solid to gas without first changing into a liquid. The solid element iodine sublimes.

subsonic
speeds below the speed of sound.

substance
matter that can be identified by name. Sand, water and oxygen are examples of substances.

succession
a series of successive plant communities that live in an environment over a period of time. The slopes of a volcano become inhabited by a series of communities after an eruption. Algae and lichen are usually the first plants. These are followed by grasses, which after a few years are replaced by shrubs. Trees eventually replace the shrubs.

sucrose [sewk-rohz]
a sugar found in plants such as sugar cane. A molecule of sucrose is made up from one molecule of glucose joining up with a molecule of a similar sugar called fructose. The formula of sucrose is $C_{12}H_{22}O_{11}$.

sugar
a type of solid crystalline carbohydrate that dissolves in water and has a sweet taste. Sugars include glucose and fructose from fruit, sucrose from sugar cane and lactose from milk.

sulphur
symbol S. A yellow, non-metallic element (Z=16). An essential element in organisms.

sulphur dioxide
a colourless, choking gas with a formula of SO_2. It is released from volcanoes and by the combustion of impure fossil fuels. See **acid rain**.

sulphuric acid [sul-fewr-ik]
a strong acid with a formula of H_2SO_4. It is used in the manufacture of paints, fertilizers and plastics.

Sun
the star in our solar system. It is a typical star of intermediate size and brightness. Sunlight and other radiation are produced by the nuclear fusion of hydrogen atoms into helium in the Sun's interior. The Sun has been in this stage of its life for 4.5 billion years. There is enough hydrogen left in the Sun to last another 4.5 billion years. When all the hydrogen in the Sun is used up, it will begin to use helium atoms as fuel for nuclear fusion. At this stage, the Sun will expand to over 10 000 times its present size. It will become a red giant star, whose outer surface will be beyond the present orbit of the Earth. It will remain a red giant star for less that half a billion years. The Sun is too small to then become a nova or a supernova. Instead it will shrink to a white dwarf star about the size of the Earth and will slowly cool for several billion years. See **red giant, sunspot, solar flare, solar wind, white dwarf**. See also **Fig. 41** (p. 140).

sunspots
dark spots on the surface of the Sun first observed by Chinese astronomers more than 2000 years ago. The numbers and size of the sunspots increase and decrease over an 11-year cycle. Scientists do not yet fully understand the causes or effects of sunspots.

supernova
a star whose brightness suddenly increases over a million times because of an explosion. The brightness lasts for several years. It is estimated that there is a supernova explosion in our galaxy every 30 years but only six have been observed in the last 1000 years. See **Fig. 41** (p. 140).

supersonic
speeds faster than the speed of sound.

surface tension
an inwards pull at the surface of a liquid that makes it behave as if it has a skin. Surface tension causes the spherical shapes of drops, and allows some small insects to walk on water. It is caused by the molecules of the liquid attracting each other.

suspension
a mixture in which small bits of an undissolved substance are spread evenly throughout a liquid.

sweat
a dilute solution of sodium chloride and urea that is produced by the sweat glands in the skin of mammals. Evaporation of sweat from the skin helps to keep the body cool.

sweat glands
small glands in the skin of mammals that secrete sweat.

switch
a device that can cut off the flow of the electric current in a circuit.

symbiosis [sim-bi-oh-sis]
when two organisms of different species benefit from living with each other. For example, the bacteria that live in the root nodules of legumes help the plants by producing nitrogen compounds that the plant can use. The nodules in the roots provide a safe place for the bacteria to live.

symbol
an abbreviation, of one or two letters, that stands for the name of something, e.g. the name of an element or a unit of measurement. See **Appendices 2** and **3**.

synapse [sy-naps]
where two nerves join.

syncline [sin-klyn]
see **fold**.

synovial capsule [sy-**noh**-vi-al]
a bag-like membrane that surrounds two bones that move in a joint. The synovial capsule contains a slippery liquid called synovial fluid that lubricates the joint.

synovial fluid
see **synovial capsule**.

synthesis [sin-thi-sis]
the making of a chemical compound from elements or from simpler compounds.

syphilis [sif-i-lis]
a sexually transmitted disease caused by a spiral-shaped bacterium. It can be treated using antibiotics.

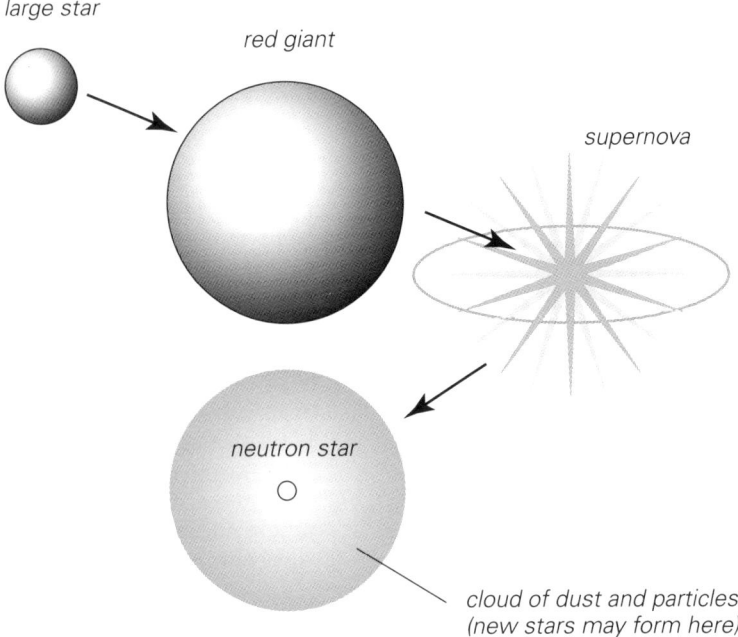

Fig. 41 the 'death' of a large star as it uses up its nuclear fuel may result in a supernova.

tap root
a root system where the smaller roots (lateral roots) grow from a main root. See **root system**.

taste bud
a small sense organ that detects taste. In land animals, the taste buds are found in the tongue. They are sensitive to four types of taste: sweet, sour, salt and bitter.

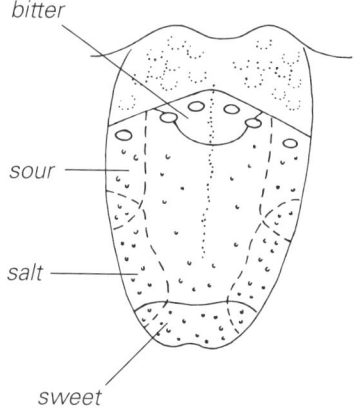

Fig. 42 taste buds on the human tongue

T cell
a type of lymphocyte that provides immunity against antigens. See **lymphocyte**, **antigen**.

technology
the use of tools and machines to increase our control and understanding of the environment.

teeth
see **tooth**.

temperature
a measure of how hot or cold an object is. The common unit of temperature is the degree Celsius (°C). A thermometer is used to measure temperature. See **Kelvin**, **absolute zero**.

temporary hard water
a form of hard water caused by dissolved calcium hydrogencarbonate $Ca(HCO_3)_2$, which can be removed by boiling the water. See **hard water**.

tendon
a strong tissue that connects muscle to bone.

tendril
the thread-like part of a climbing plant that wraps around or sticks to a support.

tension
a force that pulls. A weight hanging at the end of a rope puts tension on the rope. Bending a stick causes tension on the outside of the bend.

tentacle
flexible non-jointed organ on the head of invertebrates. An octopus has eight tentacles. They are used for feeling, gripping prey or swimming.

terminal
a part at the end of any structure. The fingers are at the terminal of the hand.

terminal velocity
the maximum velocity reached by a falling object. This happens when the air resistance equals the pull of gravity.

tertiary consumer
[ter-sher-i]
see **consumer**.

testis
the reproductive organ of a male animal that produces the sperm and male sex hormones (pl. testes). See **Fig. 38** (p. 129).

tetrapod [tet-ra-pod]
an animal that has four limbs. Includes vertebrates such as birds, reptiles, amphibians and mammals.

theory
see **laws, theories and hypotheses**.

thermal decomposition
the breakdown of a chemical compound when it is heated. For example, calcium carbonate ($CaCO_3$) decomposes when heated to form calcium oxide (CaO) and carbon dioxide (CO_2).

$$CaCO_3 \rightarrow CaO + CO_2$$

thermal energy
the energy in a body, due to the movement of the atoms or particles. Increased thermal energy causes a rise in the temperature of the body or a change in its state.

thermal expansion
the increase in the size of something as its temperature rises. The expansion is caused by the increase in movement of the atoms. A thermometer uses the thermal expansion of a

liquid to indicate a rise in temperature.

thermal reactor
see **nuclear reactor**.

thermistor
an electrical component the resistance of which changes with temperature. Most thermistors are better conductors at higher temperatures.

thermocouple
a device, consisting of two different pieces of metal joined together, that generates a small amount of electricity when heated. When joined to an ammeter, a thermocouple can be used to measure very high temperatures.

thermometer
a device used to measure temperature. A liquid-in-glass thermometer contains mercury or alcohol that expands as the temperature is raised and contracts as the temperature falls. The liquid moves up and down a narrow tube that is marked with a scale.

thermonuclear reactor
see **nuclear fusion**.

thermoplastic
see **plastic**.

thermostat
a device used to maintain a steady temperature. Thermostats used to control the temperature in ovens, refrigerators and air-conditioned rooms often use a bi-metallic strip. The bending and straightening of the bi-metallic strip as it is heated or cooled is used to switch the machines on or off.

thorax
the part of the vertebrate body that contains the heart and lungs. In mammals, the thorax is protected by the ribcage. In insects, the thorax bears the wings and legs.

thrust
the force that makes an object move. In an airplane, the thrust of the engines is opposed by air resistance.

thyroid [thyr-oid]
an endocrine gland in the neck of vertebrates. It produces hormones that control the speed of chemical reactions (metabolic rate) in cells.

tidal power
electricity generated from the energy of tides in the sea. The tidal flow of water in and out of the mouth of a river is used to turn generators that produce electricity.

tide
> the regular rise and fall of the level of the oceans. Tides are caused by the gravitational pull of the Moon and, to a lesser extent, the Sun on the water in the ocean.

tin
> symbol Sn. A silvery, metallic element (Z=50). Tin is used as a thin coat to protect iron used to make cans for food. Tin is also mixed with other metals to form a number of alloys.

tissue
> a group of similar cells that work together to do a special job. Muscles, nerves and blood are all examples of tissues.

tonne [tonn]
> a unit of mass equal to 1000 kilograms.

tooth
> a small hard structure found in the mouth of vertebrates. There are four different kinds of teeth in mammals: incisor, canine, premolar and molar. The crown of a tooth is covered with a hard enamel and is above the gum. The root lies inside the gum. Most mammals have milk teeth in infancy that are later replaced by permanent teeth. See **Fig. 43**.

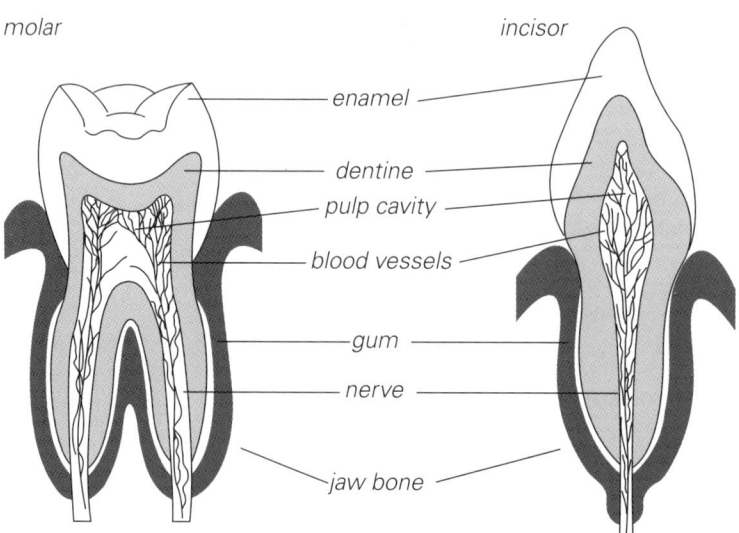

Fig. 43 human molar and incisor teeth

toxin [toks-in]
a substance made by an organism that is harmful to other organisms. Many diseases are caused by toxins given off by bacteria.

trace element
an element that is needed in very small quantities for the growth of an organism. Trace elements include iron, copper, zinc, molybdenum, manganese and boron. They are essential for most animal and plant growth.

trachea [tra-kee-a]
1 a tube in insects that carries air from openings in the body, called spiracles, to all parts of the body.
2 the large windpipe in vertebrates that carries air from the nose to the lungs. See **Fig. 25** (p. 83).

transformer
a device used to change the voltage of alternating electric current. A transformer consists of two coils of wire turned around an iron core. Current enters the input (primary) coil and causes a current to flow through the output (secondary) coil. The change in voltage depends on the number of turns of wire in the primary and secondary coils.

transistor
an electronic device used as either a switch or an amplifier. Transistors are used in all types of electronic equipment.

transition metal [tran-zi-shn]
a metal in the periodic table between Groups 2 and 3. They are generally hard and many of them form coloured salts, e.g. copper(II) sulphate is blue and iron(II) sulphate is green. Iron, copper, zinc, platinum, gold and mercury are all transition elements.

translucent [tranz-loo-sent]
describing a substance like frosted glass, through which light can pass, but through which objects cannot be seen clearly.

transparent
describing a substance like clear glass or water, through which light can pass and through which objects can be seen.

transpiration
the process by which water is lost through the leaves of a plant. Transpiration helps the water to flow up through the roots, through the stem and into the leaves.

transverse wave
wave in which the source vibrates across the direction that the wave moves. Water waves are transverse – the water moves up and down but the wave travels along. See **longitudinal wave**.

tremor
see **earthquake**.

triceps [try-seps]
the muscle that runs along the back of the upper arm. It is connected at one end to the radius and at the other to the shoulder bone (scapular). Working in opposition to the biceps, contraction of the triceps causes the arm to straighten at the elbow. See **biceps**.

tricuspid valve
[try-kus-pid]
the valve between the upper and lower chambers of the heart that stops blood flowing in the wrong direction. See **heart, atrium, ventricle**.

triple antigen [an-ti-jen]
a vaccine given to children to provide immunity against whooping cough, diphtheria and tetanus.

tropism [tro-pizm]
the growth of a plant towards or away from a stimulus. For example, roots grow towards gravity (geotropism) and shoots grow towards light (phototropism).

troposphere [tro-pers-feer]
the layer of the atmosphere closest to the Earth, containing 80% of all air.

tsunami [tsoo-**nah**-mi]
a large ocean wave caused by an undersea earthquake. Tsunamis are sometimes incorrectly called 'tidal waves'.

tumour
see **cancer**.

tungsten [tung-sten]
symbol W. A hard, grey-white metal (Z=74). It has a very high melting point and is used as the filament in electric light bulbs. It is also mixed with iron to make very hard steel.

turbine [ter-byn]
a machine in which a moving liquid or gas is used to turn a shaft. Flowing water turns the shaft of a turbine attached to a generator to make electricity in a hydroelectricity plant. Burning gases are used to turn the turbine that powers a jet engine. See **Fig. 22** (p. 75).

twins
two babies, born to the same mother at the same time. Identical twins develop from the same egg. Fraternal (non-identical) twins develop from two different eggs.

ultrasound
high frequency sound waves that can't be heard with the human ear. Ultrasound can be used to scan babies in the womb.

ultraviolet
invisible electromagnet radiation present in sunlight. Ultraviolet radiation enables vitamin D to be made in the skin. However, over-exposure to UV radiation can cause skin cancer. See **ozone layer**.

umbilical cord
[um-bi-**ly**-a-cal]
a tube that joins the foetus to the placenta. The umbilical cord is cut during birth and leaves a scar called the navel.

umbra [um-br]
the area of complete shadow caused by an eclipse. See **eclipse**, **penumbra**.

universal indicator
see **indicator**.

universe
all the space, energy and matter that exists.

uranium
[yoo-**ray**-ni-um] symbol U. A white, radioactive metallic element (Z=92). Used as a fuel in some types of nuclear reactor.

Uranus
the seventh planet in the solar system, having an orbit between Saturn and Neptune. It has about 15 natural satellites and an atmosphere of hydrogen and methane. See **Appendix 4**.

urea [yoor-i-a]
a waste substance containing nitrogen made in the liver from unwanted proteins. Dissolved in water, it passes out of the body as urine.

ureter [yoor-**ee**-terl]
the tube in mammals that carries urine from the kidney to the bladder. See **Fig. 14** (p. 53).

urethra [yoor-**ee**-thra]
the tube in mammals that carries urine from the bladder to the outside. In males it also carries semen. See **Figs. 14** (p. 53) and **38** (p. 129).

urinary bladder [yoor-in-er-i]
see **bladder**.

urinary system [yoor-in-er-i]
see **excretion**.

urine [**yoor**-in]
watery wastes removed from the blood by the kidneys. See **urea**.

uterus [**yoo**-ter-us]
the thick-walled organ in the female body where the developing embryo grows. Strong muscles in the wall of the uterus push the offspring out through the cervix and vagina during birth. See **Fig. 38** (p. 129).

vaccination
see **immunization**.

vaccine [**vak**-seen]
a substance containing disease-causing micro-organisms that have been made harmless. When injected into the body, a vaccine causes the body to make its own antibodies. See **immunize**.

vacuole [**vak**-you-ohl]
a space inside a living cell containing liquid. Plant cells often have one large vacuole. Animal cells usually have many small vacuoles. See **Fig. 7** (p. 25)

vacuum [**vak**-yoom]
a space containing very few atoms or molecules. A perfect vacuum would contain no atoms or molecules, but this is impossible to achieve in practice.

vagina [va-**jy**-na]
the tube in female mammals connecting the uterus to the outside. During sexual intercourse the male penis is placed inside the vagina. During birth the baby passes out of the uterus, through the vagina to the outside. See **Fig. 38** (p. 129).

valency [**vay**-len-si]
1 the number of electrons lost or gained by an atom to form ions.
2 the number of electrons donated by an atom to the formation of covalent bonds.

vanadium [va-**nay**-di-um]
symbol V. A silvery, white transition metal (Z=23). Oxides of vanadium are important industrial catalysts.

vapour
another word for a gas.

variable
　a factor that can be changed in an experiment to investigate its effect on the results. For example, when measuring the rate at which calcium carbonate reacts with hydrochloric acid, the variables could include the size of the calcium carbonate pieces (lumps or powder), the concentration of the acid and the temperature of the acid.

variation
　differences between individual plants or animals of the same species, e.g. height and face shape in humans. The differences can be caused by hereditary or environmental factors.

vascular system
　[**vas**-kew-ler]
　1　the network of tubes that carries fluids through the body in animals. See **circulatory system**.
　2　the system of vascular tissue in plants.

vascular tissue
　[**vas**-kew-ler]
　the system of tubes that carries water and nutrients through plants. See **phloem**, **xylem**.

vas deferens
　in vertebrates, the tube that carries the sperm away from the testes. See **Fig. 38** (p. 129).

vasectomy [va-**sek**-tom-i]
　an operation to sterilize a male by cutting the tubes (vas deferens) that carry sperm from the testes to the penis. See **sterilization**.

vector [vek-tor]
　1　a measurement that gives both magnitude (size) and also a direction. For example, force is a vector quantity. Compare **scalar**.
　2　a way in which a disease is transmitted. Mosquitoes, air, water and food are all vectors for the transmission of diseases. See **Appendix 6**.

vein
　1　a thin-walled blood vessel that carries blood towards the heart. All veins except the pulmonary vein carry deoxygenated blood.
　2　bundles of tubes in a leaf containing xylem and phloem vessels.
　3　hard tubes that strengthen the wings of insects.

velocity
　the speed of an object and the direction in which it moves. A car travelling at 40 km/h on a straight road has a constant velocity. A car travelling at 40 km/h around a corner has a changing velocity because its direction is changing. See **vector**.

venereal disease
[ve-**neer**-i-al]
See **sexually transmitted disease**.

ventricle [ven-trik-ul]
a chamber in the lower part of the heart in mammals. The right ventricle has thick muscular walls and pumps deoxygenated blood to the lungs. The left ventricle has very thick muscular walls and pumps oxygenated blood to all of the body. See **Fig. 19** (p. 67).

Venus
the second planet in the solar system, having an orbit between Mercury and Earth. It has an atmosphere of 98% carbon dioxide with the remainder being mainly nitrogen. Venus has no natural satellites. It is often called the morning or evening star because it can be seen as a bright spot in the sky. However, since it does not give out its own light, it is not really a star. See **Appendix 4**.

vertebra [ver-tib-ra]
in vertebrates, the bones that make up the vertebral column (pl. vertebrae). See **Fig. 44**.

vertebral column
in vertebrates, the flexible column made up of vertebrae from the skull to the pelvis. The spinal cord runs inside the vertebral column. The vertebral column is also called the spine, the backbone or the spinal column.

vertebrate [vert-i-brt]
an animal with a backbone. Vertebrates include birds, fish, reptiles, mammals and amphibians.

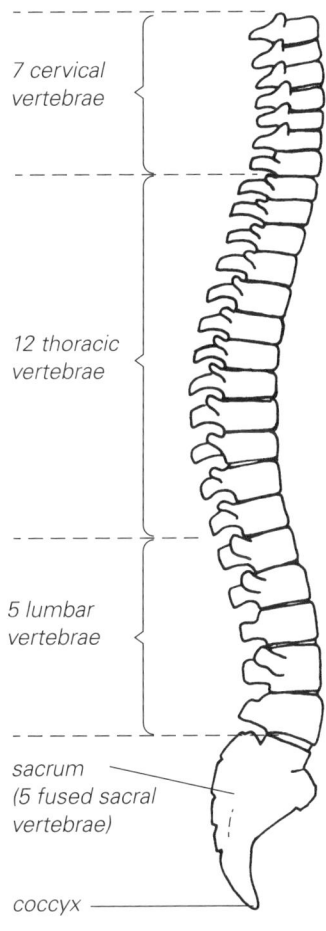

7 cervical vertebrae

12 thoracic vertebrae

5 lumbar vertebrae

sacrum (5 fused sacral vertebrae)

coccyx

Fig. 44 the human vertebral column

villus
small finger-like projections that line the small intestine (pl. villi). In humans, the villi contain blood capillaries and lymphatic vessels called lacteals that absorb the digested foods.

vinegar
see **acetic acid**.

virtual image
an image that appears to be behind a mirror or lens. Light does not pass through a virtual image so it can't be 'captured' on a screen. See **concave**.

virus
the smallest of all living micro-organisms, which can reproduce only inside cells of plants and animals. Viruses take control of the cells, which then produce more viruses. Diseases such as colds, influenza, smallpox and AIDS are caused by viruses.

viscosity [vis-cos-i-ti]
the thickness of a liquid, describing how easily it flows. Water has a low viscosity. Honey has a high viscosity. Heating a liquid decreases its viscosity.

visible spectrum
the spectrum of electromagnetic radiation, which can be 'seen' by the human eye. See **spectrum**, **electromagnetic spectrum**.

visual display unit (VDU)
a monitor connected to a computer to display words, numbers and graphics.

vitamin
an organic compound that is required by animals for their healthy growth. Some organisms can make some of the vitamins they need, e.g. humans can make vitamin D. Most vitamins must, however, be taken in through the animal's diet.

vitamin A
an organic compound that cannot be made by animals and is essential for proper sight. Vitamin A (retinol) is contained in many plants, particularly carrots and tomatoes.

vitamin B complex
a group of organic compounds that animals cannot make. B vitamins are essential for many of the important chemical reactions that take place in the body.

vitamin C
an organic compound that cannot be made by humans, but is essential for healthy cells and organ tissue. Vitamin C (ascorbic acid), is found in fruit and vegetables.

vitamin D

an organic compound that is essential for bone growth. In humans, it can be made in the skin in the presence of sunlight.

vitamin E

an organic compound that cannot be made by animals. Vitamin E (tocopherol) is essential for reproduction and is found in cereals.

vitamin K

an organic compound that cannot be made by animals. It is essential in the formation of blood clots and is available in vegetables and eggs.

vocal cords

a pair of elastic membranes found in the larynx. The cords vibrate to produce sounds when air passes through the larynx.

volatile [vol-a-tyl]

the ability of a liquid to evaporate easily. Volatile liquids have low boiling points.

volcanic rock

rock formed on the Earth's surface by the cooling and hardening of molten material (lava) from a volcano.

volt

symbol V. The measure of the voltage of a battery. The higher the voltage of a battery, the higher the electric current pushed by the battery through a circuit. See **Ohm's law**.

voltage [vohl-tij]

a measure of the amount of energy flowing between two points in an electric circuit or across the terminals of a battery. Voltage is also called the potential difference. See **volt**.

voltmeter

an instrument used to measure the voltage or potential difference across two points in an electric circuit, or across the terminals of a battery.

volume

the amount of space occupied by something. The unit of volume is the cubic metre (m^3). The volume of a liquid or the inside of a container such as a bottle is measured in cubic decimetres (dm^3) or litres. (1 dm^3 = 1 litre)

vulcanization

the process of heating raw rubber with sulphur to make it strong and flexible.

vulva

the outside opening of the vagina. In women, it is made up of two folds of flesh called labia, and the clitoris.

warm-blooded
an animal that can keep its body temperature constant. Mammals (body temperature between 36–38°C) and birds (body temperature between 38–40°C).
See **homoiotherm**.

waste product
1 any substance produced during metabolism that is of no use and is therefore excreted by the organism. See **urea**.
2 any substance produced during a chemical reaction that is of no use. See **radioactive waste**.

water
a colourless liquid. Formula H_2O. Freezing point is 0°C and boiling point is 100°C. Water is an excellent solvent.

water cycle
the movement of water between the atmosphere, the land and the sea. Rainfall wets the land and provides water for plants. Excess water runs through rivers and streams to the sea. Animals use water from rivers and streams. Water vapour moves into the atmosphere by transpiration from plants and evaporation from seas, rivers, streams, lakes and the land. The water vapour in the air condenses and falls as rain or snow.

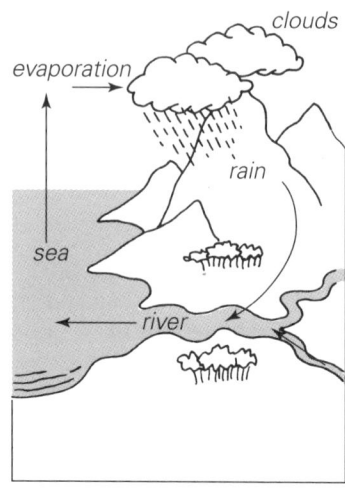

Fig. 45 the water cycle

water table
the top level of soil or rock soaked by underground water.

water vapour
the gas form of water.

watt
symbol W. The unit of power. One watt equals 1 joule of energy converted or 'used up' in one second.

wave
how forms of energy such as light, sound and water waves move from one place to another. As sound waves pass through air, they cause the particles in the air to vibrate backwards and forwards in the direction the wave is moving. This is called a longitudinal wave. The particles of air do not move along with the wave. Water waves cause water to rise and fall as the wave passes. The water does not move along with the wave. This is called a transverse wave. Electromagnetic waves such as light can also be thought of as transverse waves but they do not need air or water to move along. See **electromagnetic radiation**.

wavelength
the distance between any two wave crests or troughs. See **frequency** and **Fig. 46**.

wave power
the use of wave motion in the sea to generate electricity. Large floats are anchored in the ocean. The floats move up and down with the waves, turning a generator that produces electricity. See **renewable energy**.

weak acid
an acid that does not break up easily into hydrogen ions in solution. Acetic (ethanoic) acid CH_3COOH is a weak acid. Vinegar is a weak solution of acetic acid.

weather
a description of the condition of the atmosphere at a given time. This includes a description of the temperature, humidity, precipitation (rain, snow, hail), cloud cover, visibility and wind.

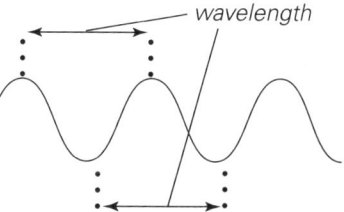

Fig. 46 wavelength

weathering

the slow breaking down of the surface of rocks into smaller particles. Physical weathering is caused by the abrasive action of wind and rain, heating and cooling, and frost action. Chemical weathering is caused by reactions with acidic rain.

weight

the downwards pull on an object, caused by the attraction of the gravitational field on its mass. The unit of weight is the newton (N). The strength of the gravitational field of the Earth is about 10 N/kg. Therefore a mass of 1 kg has a weight of 10 N on Earth. The gravitational force on the Moon is about 1.6 N/kg. Therefore a mass of 1 kilogram weighs 1.6 N on the Moon.

white blood cell

see **leucocyte**.

white dwarf

a small star that has used up all its fuel and has shrunk under the force of its own gravity.

wind

movement of air across the Earth's surface from regions of high pressure to regions of low pressure. Winds occur because some parts of the Earth's surface, such as the regions near the equator, are heated more than others. Warm air is at a lower pressure than cold air.

windpipe

see **trachea**.

wind power

the use of wind to turn generators and produce electricity. See **renewable energy**.

wing

a structure evolved by birds, insects and a few mammals (e.g. bats) that enables them to fly. See **flight**.

work

the unit of work is a joule, the same unit as energy. Work is done when a force moves. One joule of work is done when a force of 1 newton moves 1 metre.

work done = force × distance moved

X-chromosome
one of the chromosomes that determines the sex of a child. Females have two Y-chromosomes in each cell. Males have one Y- and one X-chromosome.

xenon [zen-on]
symbol Xe. A colourless, odourless noble gas (Z=54).

X-ray
a type of high energy electromagnetic radiation. X-rays can pass through many forms of matter and are used in medicine and industry to examine internal structures.

xylem [zy-lem]
part of the vascular system in plants. Hollow tubes conduct water and dissolved minerals from the roots to the leaves. The tubes are formed by cells joining together in long chains. The xylem also provides support to the plant. See **Fig. 24** (p. 80).

Y-chromosome
one of the chromosomes that determines sex in humans. See **X-chromosome**.

yeast
a group of single-celled fungi that multiply asexually by budding. Yeast uses anaerobic respiration to break down sugars into carbon dioxide and ethanol. Yeast is used in baking and brewing. See **fermentation**.

Z

symbol for the atomic number of an element. The atomic number is equal to the number of protons in an atom of the particular element. See **atomic number** and **Appendix 2**.

zinc

symbol Zn. A blue-white metallic element ($Z=30$). Used to protect iron and steel from rusting. Also used in a number of alloys. See **alloys**, **brass**, **bronze**, **galvanized iron**.

zone of influence

see **field**.

zygote [zy-goht]

a fertilized cell formed when the nucleus of a sperm or pollen grain combines with the nucleus of an ovum or ovule. See **fertilization**.

Appendix I   The periodic table of elements

Group number	1	2													3	4	5	6	7	0
							^{1}H$_{1}$													^{4}He$_{2}$
	^{7}Li$_{3}$	^{9}Be$_{4}$												^{11}B$_{5}$	^{12}C$_{6}$	^{14}N$_{7}$	^{16}O$_{8}$	^{19}F$_{9}$	^{20}Ne$_{10}$
	^{23}Na$_{11}$	^{24}Mg$_{12}$					← transition elements →							^{27}Al$_{13}$	^{28}Si$_{14}$	^{31}P$_{15}$	^{32}S$_{16}$	^{35}Cl$_{17}$	^{40}Ar$_{18}$
	^{39}K$_{19}$	^{40}Ca$_{20}$	^{45}Sc$_{21}$	^{48}Ti$_{22}$	^{51}V$_{23}$	^{52}Cr$_{24}$	^{55}Mn$_{25}$	^{56}Fe$_{26}$	^{59}Co$_{27}$	^{59}Ni$_{28}$	^{64}Cu$_{29}$	^{65}Zn$_{30}$	^{70}Ga$_{31}$	^{73}Ge$_{32}$	^{75}As$_{33}$	^{79}Se$_{34}$	^{80}Br$_{35}$	^{84}Kr$_{36}$
	^{85}Rb$_{37}$	^{88}Sr$_{38}$	^{89}Y$_{39}$	^{91}Zr$_{40}$	^{93}Nb$_{41}$	^{96}Mo$_{42}$	^{99}Tc$_{43}$	^{101}Ru$_{44}$	^{103}Rh$_{45}$	^{106}Pd$_{46}$	^{108}Ag$_{47}$	^{112}Cd$_{48}$	^{115}In$_{49}$	^{119}Sn$_{50}$	^{122}Sb$_{51}$	^{128}Te$_{52}$	^{127}I$_{53}$	^{131}Xe$_{54}$
	^{133}Cs$_{55}$	^{137}Ba$_{56}$	^{139}La$_{57}$	^{178}Hf$_{72}$	^{181}Ta$_{73}$	^{184}W$_{74}$	^{186}Re$_{75}$	^{190}Os$_{76}$	^{192}Ir$_{77}$	^{195}Pt$_{78}$	^{197}Au$_{79}$	^{201}Hg$_{80}$	^{204}Tl$_{81}$	^{207}Pb$_{82}$	^{209}Bi$_{83}$	^{210}Po$_{84}$	^{210}At$_{85}$	^{222}Rn$_{86}$
	^{223}Fr$_{87}$	^{226}Ra$_{88}$	^{227}Ac$_{89}$ *																

Elements not shown:
- 58–71 Lathanoid series
* 90–103 Actinoid series

Key

^{a}X$_{b}$

a = relative atomic mass
X = symbol
b = atomic (proton) number

Appendix 2 The elements listed in alphabetical order

element	symbol	atomic number Z	relative atomic mass	element	symbol	atomic number Z	relative atomic mass
Actinium	Ac	89	227	Einsteinium	Es	99	254
Aluminium	Al	13	27	Erbium	Er	68	167
Americium	Am	95	243	Europium	Eu	63	152
Antimony	Sb	51	122	Fermium	Fm	100	253
Argon	Ar	18	40	Fluorine	F	9	19
Arsenic	As	33	75	Francium	Fr	87	223
Astatine	At	85	210	Gadolinium	Gd	64	157
Barium	Ba	56	137	Gallium	Ga	31	70
Berkelium	Bk	97	249	Germanium	Ge	32	73
Beryllium	Be	4	9	Gold	Au	79	197
Bismuth	Bi	83	209	Hafnium	Hf	72	178.5
Boron	B	5	11	Helium	He	2	4
Bromine	Br	35	80	Holmium	Ho	67	165
Cadmium	Cd	48	112	Hydrogen	H	1	1
Caesium	Cs	55	133	Indium	In	49	115
Calcium	Ca	20	40	Iodine	I	53	127
Californium	Cf	98	251	Iridium	Ir	77	192
Carbon	C	6	12	Iron	Fe	26	56
Cerium	Ce	58	140	Krypton	Kr	36	84
Chlorine	Cl	17	35.5	Lanthanum	La	57	139
Chromium	Cr	24	52	Lawrencium	Lw	103	257
Cobalt	Co	27	59	Lead	Pb	82	207
Copper	Cu	29	64	Lithium	Li	3	7
Curium	Cm	96	247	Lutetium	Lu	71	175
Dysprosium	Dy	66	162	Magnesium	Mg	12	24

(continued on next page …)

Appendix 2 The elements listed in alphabetical order

element	symbol	atomic number Z	relative atomic mass
Manganese	Mn	25	55
Mendelevium	Md	103	256
Mercury	Hg	80	201
Molybdenum	Mo	42	96
Neodymium	Nd	60	144
Neon	Ne	10	20
Neptunium	Np	93	237
Nickel	Ni	28	59
Niobium	Nb	41	93
Nitrogen	N	7	14
Nobelium	No	102	253
Osmium	Os	76	190
Oxygen	O	8	16
Palladium	Pd	46	106
Phosphorus	P	15	31
Platinum	Pt	78	195
Plutonium	Pu	94	242
Polonium	Po	84	210
Potassium	K	19	39
Praseodymium	Pr	59	141
Promethium	Pm	61	147
Protoactinium	Pa	91	231
Radium	Ra	88	226
Radon	Rn	86	222
Rhenium	Re	75	186
Rhodium	Rh	45	103
Rubidium	Rb	37	85

element	symbol	atomic number Z	relative atomic mass
Ruthenium	Ru	44	101
Samarium	Sm	62	150
Scandium	Sc	21	45
Selenium	Se	34	79
Silicon	Si	14	28
Silver	Ag	47	108
Sodium	Na	11	23
Strontium	Sr	38	88
Sulphur	S	16	32
Tantalum	Ta	73	181
Technetium	Tc	43	99
Tellurium	Te	52	128
Terbium	Tb	65	159
Thallium	Tl	81	204
Thorium	Th	90	232
Thulium	Tm	69	169
Tin	Sn	50	119
Titanium	Ti	22	48
Tungsten	W	74	184
Uranium	U	92	238
Vanadium	V	23	51
Xenon	Xe	54	131
Ytterbium	Yb	70	173
Yttrium	Y	39	89
Zinc	Zn	30	65
Zirconium	Zr	40	91

Appendix 3 SI units

physical quantity	name	symbol
length	metre	m
mass	kilogram	kg
time	second	s
force	newton	N
pressure	Pascal	Pa
energy	joule	J
power	watt	W
temperature	Kelvin	K
frequency	hertz	Hz
voltage (potential difference)	volt	V
charge	coulomb	C
resistance	ohm	Ω

The table gives the SI units. Smaller and larger units are made by adding a prefix to the front of the base unit. For example, the prefix 'kilo' means x1000 so a kilowatt is 1000 watts. The unit is written kW. The table below gives some examples. (Note that the base unit for mass is the gram but the SI unit is the kilogram.)

multiple of unit	name and symbol	example
× 1 000 000	mega (M)	6 000 000W = 6 MW
× 1000	kilo (k)	2000Hz = 2 kHz
× 1/10	deci (d)	1/10 m = 1 dm
× 1/100	centi (c)	7/100 m = 7 cm
× 1/1000	milli (m)	3/1000 V = 3 mV
× 1/1 000 000	micro (μ)	1/1 000 000 C = 1 μC

Appendix 4 The solar system

Planet	Diameter (km)	Mass compared with Earth	Average distance from Sun (millions of km)	Revolution around Sun ('year')	Rotation ('day')	Surface temperature (approximate)
Mercury	4 878	0.06	57.9	88 days	59 days	−183°C to +380°C
Venus	12 100	0.8	108	224.7 days	243 days	450°C
Earth	12 756	1	149.6	365.26 days	23 hours 56 mins	−50°C to +50°C
Mars	6 762	0.1	227.9	687 days	24 hours 37 mins	−123°C to +26°C
Jupiter	142 700	318	778.3	11.86 years	9 hours 50 mins	−120°C
Saturn	120 800	95	1430	29.45 years	10 hours 14 mins	−133°C
Uranus	51 800	15	2869.6	84.01 years	11 hours	−220°C
Neptune	49 400	17	4496	164.8 years	16 hours	−220°C
Pluto	2 300	0.002	5900	247.7 years	6 days 9 hours	−220°C

Appendix 5 History of biotechnology

10000 BC	Neolithic men and women ate fermented grain.
6000 BC	Babylonians used yeast to make beer.
4000 BC	Egyptians used yeast to make bread dough rise.
2000 BC	The Chinese developed the fermentation process.
1400 AD	Distillation of wines and spirits was widespread.
1500	Aztecs harvested algae from lakes for food.
1686	Leeuwenhoek observed microbes through a microscope.
c. 1870	Pasteur proved that microbes were responsible for fermentation and for the decomposition of food.
c. 1890	Alcohol was first used as fuel.
1897	Buchner discovered that enzymes in yeast are responsible for converting sugar into alcohol.
1912	Microbes were first used in sewage works.
1912	Weizmann used bacteria to produce acetone (propanone) and butanol by fermentation.
1928	Fleming discovered penicillin.
1943	Avery shows that DNA carries genetic information.
1944	Chain & Florey develop large-scale production of penicillin.
1953	Watson, Crick and Franklin discover the structure of DNA.
1961	The genetic code was cracked.
1972	The first gene cloning was carried out.
1973	Brazil introduced its National Fuel Alcohol Programme.
1975	Kohler and Milstein first produced monoclonal antibodies.
1976	Guidelines on genetic engineering were drawn up.
1977	The first human gene was cloned.
1982	Human insulin was made by genetic engineering.
1987	Field trials of the first genetically engineered microbes.
1988	Genetic 'fingerprinting' techniques were developed.
1997	First mammal produced by cloning – 'Dolly' the sheep born.

Appendix 6   Diseases: causes and vectors

Disease	Cause	Vector
AIDS	Virus	Blood, semen and vaginal fluids
Amoebic dysentery	Protozoan	Food
Anaemia	Vitamin deficiency	none
Athlete's foot	Fungus	Contact
Chicken pox	Virus	Air and contact
Cholera	Bacteria	Water
Common cold	Virus	Air
Diphtheria	Bacteria	Air
Gastroenteritis	Bacteria	Food and water
German measles	Virus	Air
Gonorrhoea	Bacteria	Sexual contact
Infectious hepatitis	Virus	Water, food and body fluids
Influenza (flu)	Virus	Air
Malaria	Protozoan	Mosquitoes
Measles	Virus	Droplet
Mumps	Virus	Droplet
Plague	Bacteria	Rats and fleas
Pneumonia	Bacteria	Air
Poliomyelitis (Polio)	Virus	Water, food and possibly contact
Rabies	Virus	Dog bite
Rickets	Vitamin deficiency	none
Ringworm	Fungus	Contact
Scabies	Mite	Contact
Smallpox	Virus	Air and contact
Syphilis	Bacteria	Sexual contact
Tapeworm	Flatworm	Food
Tetanus	Bacteria	Contact of wound with soil
Threadworm	Roundworm	By mouth, either directly or on food
Tuberculosis (TB)	Bacteria	Air, infected food
Typhoid	Bacteria	Water, food
Whooping cough	Bacteria	Droplet

Notes

Notes

Notes

Notes